Betty Crocker's

New Microwaving for 1 or 2

Prentice Hall

New York   London   Toronto   Sydney   Tokyo   Singapore

Credits

Prentice Hall

Vice-President and Publisher: Anne M. Zeman
Senior Editor: Rebecca W. Atwater
Designer: Frederick J. Latasa
Editorial Assistant: Rachel A. Simon
Production Editor: Philip Metcalf

General Mills, Inc.

Editor: Karen Couné
Recipe Development and Testing: Mary Hallin Johnson, Diane Undis,
    Recipes Unlimited, Inc.
Recipe Copy Editors: Charlotte Gulden, Lauren Long
Editorial Assistant: Pam Jones
Food Stylists: Cindy Lund, Katie W. McElroy
Photographer: Nanci E. Doonan
Photography Assistant: Chuck Carver
Director, Betty Crocker Food and Publications Center: Marcia Copeland
Assistant Manager, Publications: Lois Tlusty

Prentice Hall
15 Columbus Circle
New York, New York 10023

Library of Congress Cataloging-in-Publication Data

Crocker, Betty.
    [New microwaving for 1 or 2]
    Betty Crocker's new microwaving for 1 or 2.—1st ed.
        p.   cm.

    Includes index.
    1. Microwave cookery.   2. Cookery for one.   3. Cookery
for two.   I. Title.   II. Title: New Microwaving for 1 or 2.
TX832.C77   1990   641.5′61   89-8770
ISBN 0-13-073685-6

Manufactured in the United States of America

10 9 8 7 6 5 4 3 2 1

First Prentice Hall Edition

Contents

Introduction

The microwave oven is the answer to preparing solo meals, for everyday or for special occasions. We're talking about real meals, too. There are more than 130 quick recipes, such as Beef Burgundy in seven minutes, Turkey Tenderloin with Stuffing in nine. There's even a whole chapter—On Your Own—with complete meals you can make on one plate. Think about that in terms of cleanup as well as preparation time. And there's no waste, no leftovers—except in Chapter 2. There, in "One Meal Leads to Another," you'll discover menus with built-in leftovers to be presented in a whole new manner and make the next day's dinner even speedier.

You'll find poultry and meat, of course, but you might not anticipate surprising desserts like Hot Fudge Sundae Cake. To soothe your conscience as well as satisfy your appetite, there are dozens of healthy and quick fish and vegetable dishes—delicate treats that are treated especially for the microwave. As you'd expect, all recipes come with Betty Crocker's easy-to-follow instructions.

If you're new to microwave cooking, you'll find all the facts you need in our Microwaving Tips, glossary of terms and techniques and inventory of microwave utensils.

You'll get the hang of it in no time. And no time is the essence of microwaving. The less time spent cooking and cleaning, the more time you'll have to relax and enjoy your meals. We're very sure you'll enjoy each and every one.

—THE BETTY CROCKER EDITORS

Fruited Pork (page 70)

Microwave Basics

Testing for This Book

These recipes were tested using countertop microwave ovens with power outputs of 500 to 700 watts. Refer to the use and care booklet that came with your microwave oven or contact the manufacturer to learn what the wattages are for each setting on your microwave. Power level settings are not repeated in recipes, unless a different container is used. It is always stated, with the recipe, when power levels do change.

Microwave Setting	Percentage of Power Output
High	100
Medium-high	70
Medium	50
Medium-low	30
Low	10

Special features and accessories (browning grill, microwave shelf, temperature probe, memory, etc.) vary from brand to brand. Consult your use and care booklet for guidelines on how to use these special features.

Microwaving Tips

High Altitude

Microwave cooking at high altitude (3,500 to 6,500 feet elevation), like its conventional counterpart, requires special considerations. As a general rule most recipes will use similar high altitude adjustments for microwaving as for conventional preparation. Contact the Home Service Department of the local utility company or the State Extension Office for help in solving specific problems and for recipe booklets. Recipes are also available from Colorado State University, Fort Collins, Colorado 80521.

Melting

Caramels

Place 24 caramel candies (7 ounces) and 1 tablespoon water in 10-ounce custard cup. Microwave uncovered on high (100%), stirring every 30 seconds, until melted, 1½ to 2½ minutes; stir until smooth.

Chocolate Chips

Place ¼ cup chocolate chips in 6-ounce custard cup. Microwave uncovered on medium (50%) until softened, 1 to 1½ minutes; stir until smooth.

Chocolate Squares

Place 1 square (1 ounce) chocolate in 6-ounce custard cup. Microwave uncovered on medium (50%) 1 minute; stir. Microwave uncovered until softened, 30 to 60 seconds longer.

Softening

Brown Sugar

Cover tightly and microwave on high (100%), checking every 30 seconds, until softened.

Cream Cheese

Remove foil wrapper from 3-ounce package of cream cheese and place in bowl. Microwave uncovered on medium (50%) until softened, 30 to 45 seconds. (Cheese will hold its shape as it softens.)

Hard Ice Cream

Remove the cover from 1 pint of solidly frozen ice cream; place pint of ice cream on plate. Cover with plastic wrap and microwave on high (100%) until softened, 10 to 15 seconds.

Margarine or Butter

Microwave margarine or butter uncovered on serving dish on medium-low (30%), checking every 10 seconds, until softened.

Toasting

Almonds

Place 2 tablespoons sliced almonds and 1 teaspoon margarine in 6-ounce custard cup. Microwave uncovered on high (100%), stirring every 30 seconds, until almonds are light brown, 1½ to 3 minutes. Watch carefully to prevent overbrowning.

Bread Crumbs

Toss ½ cup soft bread crumbs (about 1 slice bread) and ½ teaspoon margarine or butter, melted, in pie plate. Microwave uncovered on high (100%), stirring every 30 seconds, until toasted, 1 to 1¼ minutes.

Coconut

Place ¼ cup flaked or shredded coconut in pie plate. Microwave uncovered on high (100%), stirring every 30 seconds, until toasted, 30 to 45 seconds. Watch carefully to prevent overbrowning.

Croutons

Arrange ½ cup ½-inch bread cubes in pie plate. Microwave uncovered on high (100%) 1 minute; stir. Microwave uncovered until dry, 30 to 60 seconds longer.

Cooking Bacon

TIMETABLE

Slices	Minutes
1 to 2	¾ to 2
3	2¼ to 3
4	3 to 4
5	3¾ to 5
6	4 to 6

Microwave on high (100%) on plate lined with 2 paper towels. Cover with paper towel before microwaving.

Microwavable Utensils

Many of the recipes in this book are mixed, microwaved and served in one small casserole. Check your kitchen for microwavable utensils that are the right size for small amounts of food because a small quantity of food may not microwave well in a utensil that is too large. Although you don't need all of these sizes, a variety of utensils is helpful.

Microwavable Utensil	Size for 1 Serving	Size for 2 Servings
Casserole	10, 12, 14, 16 ounces	20, 22, 24 ounces
		1, 1½ quarts
Custard cup	6, 10 ounces	
Loaf dish		7½ × 3¾ × 2¼ inch
Measure	1 cup	2, 4 cup
Pie plate	4¼ × 1¼, 5 × 1 inch	6 × 1, 8 × 1¼, 9 × 1¼ inch
Rack	Rack to fit rectangular dish (bacon rack, roasting rack)	
Rectangular dish		10 × 6 × 1½, 11 × 7 × 1½ inch
Ring dish	2½ cup	6 cup
Round dish		8 × 1½ inch
Square dish		8 × 8 × 2 inch
Soup bowl	12, 15 ounces	
Quiche dish	10 ounces	

Use nonmetal utensils: glassware, paper, plasticware, dishwasher-safe plastic containers, ceramic plates and casseroles containing no metals, and china with no metal—that includes gold or silver—trim.

To test utensils for microwave use, place the utensil in question in the microwave beside 1 cup cool water in a glass measure. Microwave uncovered on high (100%) one minute. If the water is warm and the utensil—a dish, for example—is cool, the dish can be used for microwaving. However, if the water stayed at the same temperature and the dish feels warm, it should not be used for microwaving.

Look for microwave- and dishwasher-safe utensils that are lightweight, with handles that can be gripped with potholders and shapes that store and stack easily. If utensils are resistant to direct heat, they can also be used for conventional cooking.

Avoid metal utensils: They are not suitable for microwaving because arcing (causing a flash as in welding) can occur. Some manufacturers suggest using small pieces of aluminum foil to "shield" areas of foods that might be cooking too quickly (for example, while defrosting, chicken wing tips may begin to cook; corners of bar cookies may overcook). Follow your microwave manufacturer's directions in regard to using aluminum foil or foil-lined containers.

Paper is good for brief reheating. Use only products that are designated "microwavable." Microwavable paper towels are excellent for reheating rolls or muffins, for absorbing grease or preventing spatter. For cooking, durable paper board containers are available in many shapes and sizes.

A Glossary of Microwaving Terms and Techniques

Arrange. Foods such as muffins, potatoes or appetizers cook more evenly in a circle because all sides of food are exposed to equal amounts of microwaves.

Coat. Foods such as chicken or fish can be coated with paprika or crumbs before microwaving to add color, crispness and flavor.

Cover loosely. Use waxed paper or casserole lid slightly ajar to allow some moisture and steam to escape and to prevent spattering.

Cover tightly. Use casserole lid, plate or vented plastic wrap to speed cooking and prevent spattering.

Cover with vented plastic wrap. Use plastic wrap with one corner or edge turned back to prevent wrap from splitting.

Elevate. Foods such as quiche should be microwaved on an inverted dinner plate or on a rack so that bottom center can absorb microwaves to ensure even cooking.

Let stand. Foods such as meats, layered casseroles and some vegetables require standing time after microwaving (see individual recipes) to complete cooking and develop the flavor.

Prick. Foods such as egg yolks, potatoes or squash should be pricked with a fork before microwaving to prevent bursting.

Rearrange. Reposition food in dish so that it cooks more evenly. Move food from outside to inside and vice versa. This technique is important for food that cannot be stirred, such as kabobs.

Reheat. Foods that need long reheating times should be placed at the outside edge of the dish, and foods that need shorter reheating times (such as a roll or muffin) should be placed in the center or added later for a brief time. Spread food out, add sauce or gravy and cover to heat evenly.

Rotate. A dish can be rotated ¼ to ½ turn, as directed in recipes. Foods that cannot be stirred, such as asparagus or broccoli spears, cook more evenly when dish is rotated.

Stir. Always stir from outside to center to distribute heat and help food cook more quickly and evenly. Food heats and cooks faster on the outside.

Turn over. Foods such as small roasts or pork chops should be turned over from top to bottom for even cooking.

One Meal Leads to Another

Sweet-and-Sour Meatballs Dinner

ONE MEAL

*Sweet-and-Sour Meatballs

*Fluffy Rice

*Sesame Carrots

*Chocolate-frosted Cupcakes

FOR PERFECT TIMING

1. Prepare Chocolate-frosted Cupcakes.
2. Prepare Fluffy Rice.
3. Prepare Sweet-and-Sour Meatballs.
4. Prepare Sesame Carrots.
5. Reheat rice 1 to 1½ minutes.

*Recipe included

Fluffy Rice

1 SERVING

¾ cup uncooked instant rice

¾ cup water

¼ teaspoon salt

1 teaspoon margarine or butter

Place all ingredients in 16-ounce casserole. Cover tightly and microwave on high (100%) until boiling, 2½ to 3 minutes. Let stand covered 5 minutes; fluff with fork. Refrigerate ¾ cup rice; use within 2 days for Meatballs with Spanish Rice (page 14) or Easy Fried Rice (page 21).

2 SERVINGS

1½ cups uncooked instant rice

1½ cups water

½ teaspoon salt

2 teaspoons margarine or butter

Place all ingredients in 1-quart casserole. Cover tightly and microwave on high (100%) until boiling, 4½ to 5 minutes. Let stand covered 5 minutes; fluff with fork. Refrigerate 1½ cups rice; use within 2 days for Meatballs with Spanish Rice (page 14) or Easy Fried Rice (page 21).

Sweet-and-Sour Meatballs Dinner

Chocolate-frosted Cupcakes

1 SERVING

Prepare Chocolate-frosted Cupcakes for 2 Servings. Wrap 1 unfrosted cupcake; use within 2 days for Fruit Trifle (page 16). Wrap and freeze remaining unfrosted cupcakes for another meal.

2 SERVINGS

½ package (10¼-ounce size) microwave yellow cake mix with chocolate frosting (¾ cup)
¼ cup water
2 tablespoons vegetable oil
2 tablespoons beaten egg

Line 4 medium muffin cups, 2½ × 1¼ inches, with paper baking cups. Or arrange four 6-ounce custard cups in circle on 12-inch plate. Mix all ingredients except frosting with fork in bowl until moistened, about 1 minute. Divide batter evenly among muffin cups. Microwave uncovered on high (100%) until tops spring back when touched lightly and are almost dry, 1¼ to 1½ minutes. Let stand uncovered 1 minute; remove from cups. Cool on wire rack. Wrap 2 cupcakes; use within 2 days for Fruit Trifle (page 16).

Knead frosting packet about 10 seconds. Cut off one corner of packet; squeeze about 1 tablespoon frosting onto each cupcake. Spread frosting over cupcake. Wrap frosting packet and refrigerate for use with remaining cake mix.

Sesame Carrots

1 SERVING

¾ cup ¼-inch-thick strips carrot (2 inches long)
1 teaspoon water
1 teaspoon margarine or butter
Dash of salt
Dash of sesame seed

Place carrots and water in 8-ounce casserole. Cover tightly and microwave on high (100%) until crisp-tender, 2½ to 3 minutes; drain. Stir in remaining ingredients.

2 SERVINGS

1½ cups ¼-inch-thick strips carrot (2 inches long)
2 teaspoons water
2 teaspoons margarine or butter
⅛ teaspoon salt
⅛ teaspoon sesame seed

Place carrots and water in 16-ounce casserole. Cover tightly and microwave on high (100%) until crisp-tender, 4 to 5 minutes; drain. Stir in remaining ingredients.

Sweet-and-Sour Meatballs

1 SERVING

½ pound ground beef
1 tablespoon dry bread crumbs
1 tablespoon chopped onion
1 tablespoon catsup
2 tablespoons beaten egg
1 small green pepper, cut into 1-inch pieces
½ can (8-ounce size) pineapple chunks in juice, drained, half the juice reserved
1 teaspoon cornstarch
1 teaspoon packed brown sugar
1 teaspoon soy sauce

Mix ground beef, bread crumbs, onion, catsup and egg; shape into ten 1¼-inch balls. Place meatballs in 1-quart casserole. Cover with waxed paper and microwave on high (100%) 1½ minutes; rotate casserole ½ turn. Sprinkle green pepper over meatballs. Cover with waxed paper and microwave until meatballs are no longer pink inside, 1½ to 2 minutes longer; drain.

Remove half the meatballs and green pepper; refrigerate and use within 2 days for Meatballs with Spanish Rice (page 14).

Mix pineapple, reserved juice, the cornstarch, brown sugar and soy sauce. Stir into remaining meatballs in casserole. Microwave uncovered until sauce thickens and boils, 1½ to 2 minutes.

2 SERVINGS

1 pound ground beef
2 tablespoons dry bread crumbs
2 tablespoons chopped onion
2 tablespoons catsup
1 egg, beaten
1 medium green pepper, cut into 1-inch pieces
1 can (8 ounces) pineapple chunks in juice, undrained
2 teaspoons cornstarch
2 teaspoons packed brown sugar
2 teaspoons soy sauce

Mix ground beef, bread crumbs, onion, catsup and egg; shape into twenty 1¼-inch balls. Place meatballs in 8 × 1½-inch dish. Cover with waxed paper and microwave on high (100%) 3 minutes; rotate dish ½ turn. Sprinkle green pepper over meatballs. Cover with waxed paper and microwave until meatballs are no longer pink inside, 2½ to 3 minutes longer; drain.

Remove half the meatballs and green pepper; refrigerate and use within 2 days for Meatballs with Spanish Rice (page 14).

Mix pineapple, cornstarch, brown sugar and soy sauce. Stir into remaining meatballs in dish. Microwave uncovered until sauce thickens and boils, 3½ to 4 minutes.

MEATBALLS WITH SPANISH RICE DINNER

ANOTHER MEAL

Meatballs with Spanish Rice

Relishes

Dinner Roll

Fruit Trifle

FOR PERFECT TIMING

1. Prepare Fruit Trifle.
2. Prepare desired relishes, such as pickled peppers, marinated artichoke hearts, radishes or olives.
3. Prepare Meatballs with Spanish Rice.
4. Warm dinner roll.

*Recipe included

Meatballs with Spanish Rice

1 SERVING

5 cooked meatballs and the green pepper
   from Sweet-and-Sour Meatballs (page 13)
¾ cup cooked rice from Fluffy Rice
   (page 11)
½ can (8-ounce size) whole tomatoes,
   undrained
1 tablespoon catsup
½ teaspoon sugar
¼ teaspoon chili powder

Stir all ingredients in 24-ounce casserole. Cover
tightly and microwave on high (100%) until hot,
3 to 3½ minutes.

2 SERVINGS

10 cooked meatballs and the green pepper
   from Sweet-and-Sour Meatballs (page 13)
1½ cups cooked rice from Fluffy Rice
   (page 11)
1 can (8 ounces) whole tomatoes, undrained
2 tablespoons catsup
1 teaspoon sugar
½ teaspoon chili powder

Stir all ingredients in 1-quart casserole. Cover
tightly and microwave on high (100%) until hot,
6 to 7 minutes.

Fruit Trifle (page 16)

Fruit Trifle

1 SERVING

1 cupcake from Chocolate-frosted Cupcakes (page 12)
1½ teaspoons currant jelly
3 strawberries (with stems)
½ kiwifruit, pared
2 tablespoons frozen whipped topping, thawed

Cut cupcake into ½-inch cubes; place in 6-ounce custard cup. Place jelly in another 6-ounce custard cup and microwave, uncovered on high (100%) until melted 15 to 20 seconds; spoon jelly over cake. Remove stems from 2 strawberries and slice; slice kiwifruit. Arrange sliced fruit on cake; spread with whipped topping. Slice remaining strawberry 3 or 4 times from point to, but not through, stem end; fan slices. Garnish trifle with strawberry fan.

2 SERVINGS

2 cupcakes from Chocolate-frosted Cupcakes (page 12)
1 tablespoon currant jelly
6 strawberries (with stems)
1 kiwifruit, pared
¼ cup frozen whipped topping, thawed

Cut cupcakes into ½-inch cubes; divide between two 6-ounce custard cups. Place jelly in another 6-ounce custard cup and microwave, uncovered on high (100%) until melted 20 to 30 seconds; spoon over cake. Remove stems from 4 strawberries and slice; slice kiwifruit. Arrange sliced fruit on cake; spread with whipped topping. Slice remaining strawberries 3 or 4 times from points to, but not through, stem ends; fan slices. Garnish trifle with strawberry fans.

SPINACH-STUFFED CHICKEN BREAST DINNER

ONE MEAL

Spinach-stuffed Chicken Breast

Fluffy Rice

Applesauce-Nut Gelatin Salad

Brandied Peaches

FOR PERFECT TIMING

1. Prepare Applesauce-Nut Gelatin Salad.
2. Prepare Brandied Peaches.
3. Prepare Fluffy Rice (page 11).
4. Prepare Spinach-stuffed Chicken Breast.

*Recipe included

Brandied Peaches

1 SERVING

1 can (8 ounces) peach halves, drained
1 teaspoon brandy
4 whole cloves

Place 2 peach halves, cut sides up, in 10-ounce shallow casserole. Pour ½ teaspoon brandy over each half; top with 2 cloves. Microwave uncovered on high (100%) until hot, 30 to 45 seconds. Serve warm or chilled. Cover and refrigerate remaining peach halves; use for Peach Parfait (page 21).

2 SERVINGS

1 can (16 ounces) peach halves, drained
2 teaspoons brandy
8 whole cloves

Place 4 peach halves, cut sides up, in 1-quart shallow casserole. Pour ½ teaspoon brandy over each half; top with 2 cloves. Microwave uncovered on high (100%) until hot, 1 to 1¼ minutes. Serve warm or chilled. Cover and refrigerate remaining peach halves; use for Peach Parfait (page 21).

Spinach-stuffed Chicken Breast

1 SERVING

2 boneless, skinless chicken breast halves
  (about 3 ounces each)
Dash of salt
Dash of pepper
1 package (10 ounces) frozen chopped
  spinach
2 tablespoons chopped water chestnuts
Dash of garlic salt
2 teaspoons margarine or butter
1 tablespoon shredded Swiss cheese
2 teaspoons dry bread crumbs
2 teaspoons grated Parmesan cheese
Dash of paprika

Flatten each chicken breast half to ¼-inch thickness between plastic wrap or waxed paper; sprinkle with salt and pepper.

Cut frozen spinach into fourths; wrap and freeze ¾ package spinach for another meal. Place ¼ spinach in 10-ounce casserole. Cover tightly and microwave on high (100%) until thawed, 1½ to 1¾ minutes; drain. Mix in water chestnuts and garlic salt. Spread half of the spinach filling on each chicken breast half. Roll up 1 chicken breast half; secure with wooden picks. Place margarine in shallow 24-ounce casserole. Microwave uncovered on high (100%) until melted, 30 to 40 seconds. Dip rolled chicken breast half in margarine; place in casserole with margarine.

Sprinkle Swiss cheese over filling on remaining chicken breast half; roll up. Secure with wooden picks. Mix bread crumbs, Parmesan cheese and paprika on waxed paper. Dip chicken breast half in margarine in casserole; coat with crumb mixture. Place in casserole. Cover with waxed paper and microwave on high (100%) until done,

2 SERVINGS

4 boneless, skinless chicken breast halves
  (about 3 ounces each)
Dash of salt
Dash of pepper
1 package (10 ounces) frozen chopped
  spinach
¼ cup chopped water chestnuts
⅛ teaspoon garlic salt
1 tablespoon plus 1 teaspoon margarine or
  butter
2 tablespoons shredded Swiss cheese
1 tablespoon plus 1 teaspoon dry bread
  crumbs
1 tablespoon plus 1 teaspoon grated
  Parmesan cheese
⅛ teaspoon paprika

Flatten each chicken breast half to ¼-inch thickness between plastic wrap or waxed paper; sprinkle with salt and pepper.

Cut frozen spinach into halves; wrap and freeze ½ package spinach for another meal. Place ½ package spinach in 20-ounce casserole. Cover tightly and microwave on high (100%) until thawed, 3 to 3½ minutes; drain. Mix in water chestnuts and garlic salt. Spread one-fourth of the spinach filling on each chicken breast half. Roll up 2 chicken breast halves; secure with wooden picks. Place margarine in shallow 8 × 1½-inch dish. Microwave uncovered on high (100%) until melted, 30 to 40 seconds. Dip rolled chicken breast halves in margarine; place in dish with margarine.

Sprinkle Swiss cheese over filling on remaining chicken breast halves; roll up. Secure with wooden picks. Mix bread crumbs, Parmesan

5 to 6 minutes. Remove wooden picks. Wrap and refrigerate uncoated chicken breast half; use within 2 days for Cashew Chicken with Vegetables (page 22).

cheese and paprika on waxed paper. Dip chicken breast halves in margarine in dish; coat with crumb mixture. Place in dish. Cover with waxed paper and microwave on high (100%) until done, 9 to 10½ minutes. Remove wooden picks. Wrap and refrigerate uncoated chicken breast halves; use within 2 days for Cashew Chicken with Vegetables (page 22).

Applesauce-Nut Gelatin Salad

1 SERVING

½ cup water
½ package (3-ounce size) cherry- or raspberry-flavored gelatin (3 tablespoons dry)
¼ cup water
¼ cup applesauce
1 tablespoon chopped celery
1 tablespoon chopped walnuts

Pour water into 1-cup measure. Microwave uncovered on high (100%) until boiling, 1½ to 2 minutes. Stir in gelatin until dissolved. Pour ¼ cup gelatin mixture into small bowl; stir in ¼ cup water. Cover and refrigerate until set; use for Peach Parfait (page 21).

Stir applesauce, celery and walnuts into remaining gelatin mixture. Pour into dessert dish or 8-ounce mold. Cover and refrigerate until set, about 2 hours.

2 SERVINGS

1 cup water
1 package (3 ounces) cherry- or raspberry-flavored gelatin (dry)
½ cup water
½ cup applesauce
2 tablespoons chopped celery
2 tablespoons chopped walnuts

Pour water into 2-cup measure. Microwave uncovered on high (100%) until boiling, 2½ to 3 minutes. Stir in gelatin until dissolved. Pour ½ cup gelatin mixture into small bowl; stir in ½ cup water. Cover and refrigerate until set; use for Peach Parfait (page 21).

Stir applesauce, celery and walnuts into remaining gelatin mixture. Pour into 2 dessert dishes or 8-ounce molds. Cover and refrigerate until set, about 2 hours.

CASHEW CHICKEN WITH VEGETABLES DINNER

ANOTHER MEAL

Cashew Chicken with Vegetables

Easy Fried Rice

Tossed Salad

Breadsticks

Peach Parfait

FOR PERFECT TIMING

1. Prepare Peach Parfait.
2. Prepare tossed salad.
3. Prepare Cashew Chicken and Vegetables.
4. Prepare Easy Fried Rice.

*Recipe included

Peach Parfait

1 SERVING

½ cup prepared gelatin from Applesauce-Nut Gelatin Salad (page 19)

1 peach half from Brandied Peaches (page 17)

2 tablespoons frozen (thawed) whipped topping

Unmold gelatin; cut into ½-inch cubes. Cut peach half into ¼-inch pieces. Alternately layer gelatin and peaches in dessert dish; top with whipped topping.

2 SERVINGS

1 cup prepared gelatin from Applesauce-Nut Gelatin Salad (page 19)

2 peach halves from Brandied Peaches (page 17)

¼ cup frozen (thawed) whipped topping

Unmold gelatin; cut into ½-inch cubes. Cut peach halves into ¼-inch pieces. Alternately layer gelatin and peaches in 2 dessert dishes; top with whipped topping.

Easy Fried Rice

1 SERVING

1 green onion, sliced
2 tablespoons beaten egg
¾ cup cooked rice from Fluffy Rice (page 11)
½ teaspoon soy sauce
¼ teaspoon parsley flakes

Stir onion into beaten egg in greased 8-ounce casserole. Microwave uncovered on high (100%) until egg is almost set, 30 to 40 seconds; stir to break egg into small pieces. Stir in remaining ingredients. Microwave uncovered until rice is hot, 20 to 30 seconds.

2 SERVINGS

1 egg
2 green onions, sliced
1½ cups cooked rice from Fluffy Rice (page 11)
1 teaspoon soy sauce
½ teaspoon parsley flakes

Beat egg with fork in greased 16-ounce casserole; stir in onions. Microwave uncovered on high (100%) until egg is almost set, 1 to 1¼ minutes; stir to break egg into small pieces. Stir in remaining ingredients. Microwave uncovered until rice is hot, 1 to 1¼ minutes.

Cashew Chicken with Vegetables

1 SERVING

¼ cup sliced celery

¼ cup sliced carrot

½ small clove garlic, finely chopped

1½ teaspoons margarine or butter

1 cooked chicken breast half from Spinach-stuffed Chicken Breast (page 18)

1½ teaspoons soy sauce

1 tablespoon dry sherry

¼ teaspoon cornstarch

¼ teaspoon packed brown sugar

2 teaspoons broken cashews

Place celery, carrot, garlic and margarine in 16-ounce casserole. Microwave uncovered on high (100%) until vegetables are crisp-tender, 2 to 2½ minutes. Cut chicken into ⅛-inch slices. Mix soy sauce, sherry, cornstarch and brown sugar. Stir soy sauce mixture and chicken into vegetables. Cover tightly and microwave until chicken is hot and sauce is slightly thickened, 1 to 1¼ minutes; sprinkle with cashews.

2 SERVINGS

½ cup sliced celery

½ cup sliced carrot

1 small clove garlic, finely chopped

1 tablespoon margarine or butter

2 cooked chicken breast halves from Spinach-stuffed Chicken Breast (page 18)

1 tablespoon soy sauce

2 tablespoons dry sherry

½ teaspoon cornstarch

½ teaspoon packed brown sugar

1 tablespoon broken cashews

Place celery, carrots, garlic and margarine in 1-quart casserole. Microwave uncovered on high (100%) until vegetables are crisp-tender, 3 to 3½ minutes. Cut chicken into ⅛-inch slices. Mix soy sauce, sherry, cornstarch and brown sugar. Stir soy sauce mixture and chicken into vegetables. Cover tightly and microwave until chicken is hot and sauce is slightly thickened, 1½ to 2 minutes; sprinkle with cashews.

TURKEY TENDERLOIN WITH STUFFING DINNER

ONE MEAL

Turkey Tenderloin with Stuffing

Buttered Broccoli

Fruit Salad

Chocolate and Vanilla Swirl Pudding

FOR PERFECT TIMING

1. Prepare Chocolate and Vanilla Swirl Pudding.
2. Prepare Turkey Tenderloin with Stuffing.
3. Prepare fruit salad.
4. Prepared Buttered Broccoli.

*Recipe included

Buttered Broccoli

1 SERVING

1½ cups broccoli flowerets
2 teaspoons water
½ teaspoon margarine or butter
Dash of dried tarragon

Place broccoli and water in 16-ounce casserole. Cover tightly and microwave on high (100%) until tender, 2 to 2½ minutes; drain. Cover and refrigerate half of the broccoli; use for Marinated Broccoli Salad (page 27). Stir margarine and tarragon into remaining broccoli.

2 SERVINGS

3 cups broccoli flowerets
1 tablespoon water
1 teaspoon margarine or butter
Dash of dried tarragon

Place broccoli and water in 1-quart casserole. Cover tightly and microwave on high (100%) until tender, 4 to 4½ minutes; drain. Cover and refrigerate half of the broccoli; use for Marinated Broccoli Salad (page 27). Stir margarine and tarragon into remaining broccoli.

Chocolate and Vanilla Swirl Pudding

1 SERVING

2 tablespoons sugar

1 tablespoon cornstarch

1 cup milk

2 tablespoons beaten egg

1½ teaspoons margarine or butter

½ teaspoon vanilla

1 tablespoon semisweet chocolate chips

Mix sugar and cornstarch in 2-cup measure; stir in milk and egg. Microwave uncovered on high (100%) 2 minutes; stir. Microwave uncovered until mixture thickens and boils, 1½ to 2 minutes longer; stir in margarine and vanilla. Cover and refrigerate ¾ cup pudding; use within 2 days for Fruit Pudding (page 28).

Stir chocolate chips into ¼ cup of the remaining pudding until melted. Layer vanilla and chocolate pudding alternately in parfait glass or swirl in serving dish. Refrigerate until serving time. Garnish with fresh berries or sliced almonds if desired.

2 SERVINGS

¼ cup sugar

2 tablespoons cornstarch

2 cups milk

1 egg, beaten

1 tablespoon margarine or butter

1 teaspoon vanilla

2 tablespoons semisweet chocolate chips

Mix sugar and cornstarch in 4-cup measure; stir in milk and egg. Microwave uncovered on high (100%) 3 minutes; stir. Microwave uncovered until mixture thickens and boils, 2½ to 3 minutes longer; stir in margarine and vanilla. Cover and refrigerate 1¼ cups pudding; use within 2 days for Fruit Pudding (page 28).

Stir chocolate chips into ½ cup of the remaining pudding until melted. Layer vanilla and chocolate pudding alternately in parfait glasses or swirl in serving dishes. Refrigerate until serving time. Garnish with fresh berries or sliced almonds if desired.

Chocolate and Vanilla Swirl Pudding

Turkey Tenderloin with Stuffing

1 SERVING

½ pound turkey tenderloin
⅓ cup water
1 tablespoon margarine or butter
¼ package (6-ounce size) chicken-flavored stuffing mix with seasoning packet (about ⅔ cup)

Place turkey tenderloin, water, margarine and 1 tablespoon seasoning mix from the stuffing mix in 24-ounce casserole. Cover tightly and microwave on high (100%) until thickest parts are done, 4½ to 5 minutes. Remove turkey with slotted spoon; reserve.

Stir ¾ cup of the bread cubes into liquid in casserole; cover and let stand 5 minutes. Cut half of the turkey into slices. Cover and refrigerate ½ cup of the stuffing and the uncut turkey; use within 2 days for Turkey Club Casserole (page 28). Spread remaining stuffing evenly in casserole; arrange turkey slices on top. Microwave uncovered until hot, 20 to 30 seconds.

2 SERVINGS

1 pound turkey tenderloins
¾ cup water
2 tablespoons margarine or butter
½ package (6-ounce size) chicken-flavored stuffing mix with seasoning packet (about 1¼ cups)

Place turkey tenderloins in 10 × 6 × 1½-inch dish with thickest parts to outside edges. Add water, margarine and 2 tablespoons seasoning mix from the stuffing mix. Cover tightly and microwave on high (100%) until thickest parts are done, 7 to 8 minutes. Remove turkey with slotted spoon; reserve.

Stir 1¼ cups of the bread cubes into liquid in dish; cover and let stand 5 minutes. Cut half of the turkey into slices. Cover and refrigerate ¾ cup of the stuffing and the uncut turkey; use within 2 days for Turkey Club Casserole (page 28). Spread remaining stuffing evenly in dish; arrange turkey slices on top. Microwave uncovered until hot, 30 to 40 seconds.

TURKEY CLUB CASSEROLE DINNER

ANOTHER MEAL

Turkey Club Casserole

Marinated Broccoli Salad

Fruit Pudding

FOR PERFECT TIMING

1. Prepare Marinated Broccoli Salad.
2. Prepare Turkey Club Casserole.
3. Prepare Fruit Pudding.

*Recipe included

Marinated Broccoli Salad

1 SERVING

2 tablespoons sliced carrot

1 small green onion, sliced

¾ cup cooked broccoli from Buttered Broccoli (page 23)

1 tablespoon plus 2 teaspoons Italian dressing

1 lettuce leaf

Place carrot and onion in 1-cup measure. Microwave uncovered on high (100%) until crisp-tender, 30 to 45 seconds; mix with broccoli and dressing in bowl. Cover and refrigerate until chilled. Serve on lettuce leaf.

2 SERVINGS

¼ cup sliced carrot

1 large green onion, sliced

1½ cups cooked broccoli from Buttered Broccoli (page 23)

3 tablespoons Italian dressing

2 lettuce leaves

Place carrot and onion in 1-cup measure. Microwave uncovered on high (100%) until crisp-tender, 1 to 1¼ minutes; mix with broccoli and dressing in bowl. Cover and refrigerate until chilled. Serve on lettuce leaves.

Turkey Club Casserole

1 SERVING

1 slice bacon, cut into ½-inch pieces
½ cup stuffing from Turkey Tenderloin
   with Stuffing (page 26)
Cooked turkey tenderloin from Turkey
   Tenderloin with Stuffing (page 26), cut
   into cubes
2 slices medium tomato
2 tablespoons process cheese spread

Place bacon in 1-quart casserole. Cover loosely and microwave on high (100%) until almost crisp, 1 to 2 minutes; drain and reserve.

Spread stuffing in 16-ounce shallow casserole; top with turkey and tomato. Place cheese spread in 1-cup measure. Microwave cheese spread uncovered on high (100%) until melted, 20 to 30 seconds; pour over tomato and turkey in casserole. Sprinkle with bacon. Microwave uncovered until hot, 2 to 2½ minutes.

2 SERVINGS

2 slices bacon, cut into ½-inch pieces
¾ cup stuffing from Turkey Tenderloin
   with Stuffing (page 26)
Cooked turkey tenderloin from Turkey
   Tenderloin with Stuffing (page 26), cut
   into cubes
1 small tomato, sliced
¼ cup process cheese spread

Place bacon in 1-quart casserole. Cover loosely and microwave on high (100%) until almost crisp, 2 to 3 minutes; drain. Crumble bacon and reserve.

Spread stuffing in 1-quart shallow casserole; top with turkey and tomato. Place cheese spread in 1-cup measure. Microwave cheese spread uncovered on high (100%) until melted, 45 to 60 seconds; pour over tomato and turkey in casserole. Sprinkle with bacon. Microwave uncovered until hot, 4½ to 5 minutes.

Fruit Pudding

1 SERVING

½ cup cut-up fresh fruit (berries, apple,
   banana, pear)
¾ cup pudding from Chocolate and Vanilla
   Swirl Pudding (page 25)
1 tablespoon frozen (thawed) whipped
   topping

Place fruit in serving dish. Stir pudding until creamy; spoon over fruit. Top with whipped topping.

2 SERVINGS

1 cup cut-up fresh fruit (berries, apple,
   banana, pear)
1¼ cups pudding from Chocolate and
   Vanilla Swirl Pudding (page 25)
2 tablespoons frozen (thawed) whipped
   topping

Divide fruit between 2 serving dishes. Stir pudding until creamy; spoon over fruit. Top with whipped topping.

MARINATED SALMON STEAKS DINNER

ONE MEAL

Marinated Salmon Steaks

Poppy Seed Fettuccine

Orange-glazed Peas

Dinner Roll

Quick Baked Apple

FOR PERFECT TIMING

1. Marinate salmon steaks.
2. Prepare Quick Baked Apple.
3. Prepare Poppy Seed Fettuccine.
4. Complete Marinated Salmon Steaks.
5. Prepare Orange-glazed Peas.
6. Warm dinner roll.

*Recipe included

Orange-glazed Peas

1 SERVING

½ cup frozen green peas
½ teaspoon orange marmalade

Place peas in 6-ounce custard cup. Cover tightly and microwave on high (100%) until tender, 2 to 2½ minutes. Stir in marmalade; cover to keep peas warm.

2 SERVINGS

1 cup frozen green peas
1 teaspoon orange marmalade

Place peas in 10-ounce custard cup. Cover tightly and microwave on high (100%) until tender, 3 to 3½ minutes. Stir in marmalade; cover to keep peas warm.

Marinated Salmon Steaks

1 SERVING

2 fresh or frozen (thawed) salmon steaks
   (5 to 6 ounces each)
2 tablespoons creamy cucumber dressing
1 teaspoon snipped parsley

Place salmon steaks in pie plate, 9 × 1¼ inches. Spread about ½ tablespoon dressing on each steak. Turn salmon over; spread with remaining dressing. Refrigerate uncovered 15 minutes. Cover with waxed paper and microwave on high (100%) until salmon flakes easily with fork, 5½ to 7 minutes. Sprinkle parsley over 1 salmon steak; keep warm. Cover and refrigerate remaining salmon steak; use within 2 days for Salmon Parmigiana (page 35).

2 SERVINGS

4 fresh or frozen (thawed) salmon steaks
   (5 to 6 ounces each)
¼ cup creamy cucumber dressing
2 teaspoons snipped parsley

Place salmon steaks in pie plate, 9 × 1¼ inches. Spread about ½ tablespoon dressing on each steak. Turn steaks over; spread with remaining dressing. Refrigerate uncovered 15 minutes. Cover with waxed paper and microwave on high (100%) until salmon flakes easily with fork, 6½ to 9 minutes. Sprinkle parsley over 2 salmon steaks; keep warm. Cover and refrigerate remaining salmon steaks; use within 2 days for Salmon Parmigiana (page 35).

Poppy Seed Fettuccine

1 SERVING

2 cups hot cooked fettuccine (4 ounces
   uncooked)
1 tablespoon olive oil, margarine or butter
⅛ teaspoon poppy seed

Rinse half the fettuccine in cold water; drain. Cover and refrigerate; use within 2 days for Salmon Parmigiana (page 35). Stir olive oil and poppy seed into remaining fettuccine; cover to keep warm.

2 SERVINGS

4 cups hot cooked fettuccine (8 ounces
   uncooked)
2 tablespoons olive oil, margarine or butter
¼ teaspoon poppy seed

Rinse half of the fettuccine in cold water; drain. Cover and refrigerate; use within 2 days for Salmon Parmigiana (page 35). Stir olive oil and poppy seed into remaining fettuccine; cover to keep warm.

Marinated Salmon Steaks Dinner (page 29)

Salmon Parmigiana

1 SERVING

½ cup sliced mushrooms

1½ teaspoons margarine or butter

Dash of dried dill weed

¼ cup frozen green peas

1 teaspoon all-purpose flour

1 cup cooked fettuccine from Poppy Seed Fettuccine (page 31)

2 tablespoons half-and-half or milk

1 cooked salmon steak from Marinated Salmon Steaks (page 31)

1 tablespoon grated Parmesan cheese

⅛ teaspoon garlic salt

Place mushrooms, margarine and dill weed in 24-ounce casserole. Microwave uncovered on high (100%) 1 to 1½ minutes; stir in peas and flour. Microwave uncovered until hot, 1 to 1½ minutes. Mix in fettuccine and half-and-half. Remove skin and bones from salmon. Cut salmon into 1-inch pieces; mix into fettuccine. Cover loosely and microwave 45 seconds; toss. Cover loosely and microwave until hot, 1 to 1¼ minutes longer. Mix in cheese and garlic salt.

2 SERVINGS

1 cup sliced mushrooms

1 tablespoon margarine or butter

⅛ teaspoon dried dill weed

½ cup frozen green peas

2 teaspoons all-purpose flour

2 cups cooked fettuccine from Poppy Seed Fettuccine (page 31)

¼ cup half-and-half or milk

2 cooked salmon steaks from Marinated Salmon Steaks (page 31)

2 tablespoons grated Parmesan cheese

¼ teaspoon garlic salt

Place mushrooms, margarine and dill weed in 1-quart casserole. Microwave uncovered on high (100%) 1½ to 2 minutes; stir in peas and flour. Microwave uncovered until hot, 1½ to 2 minutes. Mix in fettuccine and half-and-half. Remove skin and bones from salmon. Cut salmon into 1-inch pieces; mix into fettuccine. Cover loosely and microwave 1½ minutes; toss. Cover loosely and microwave until hot, 1½ to 2 minutes longer. Mix in cheese and garlic salt.

Salmon Parmigiana Dinner (page 33)

On Your Own

Steak au Poivre Dinner

1 medium baking potato
Salt
⅛ teaspoon black peppercorns, crushed
1 slice (3 ounces) beef tenderloin (¾ inch thick)
½ can (8-ounce size) French-style green beans, drained
¼ teaspoon sesame seed
Dash of garlic powder
1 teaspoon margarine or butter

Dampen potato with a few drops water; sprinkle with salt. Prick several times with fork to allow steam to escape. Place potato on plate. Microwave uncovered on high (100%) until almost tender, 3 to 3½ minutes.

Press peppercorns into both sides of tenderloin. Place on plate next to potato; turn potato over. Place beans on plate with beef and potato; sprinkle with sesame seed and garlic powder. Dot with margarine. Cover with waxed paper and microwave on medium (50%) until beef is done, 3½ to 4½ minutes. Top potato with seasoned sour cream if desired.

Mini–Meat Loaf Dinner

1 teaspoon margarine or butter
⅛ teaspoon dried dill weed
1 medium potato (about 6 ounces)
2 frozen half ears corn (about 2¾ inches each)
¼ pound lean ground beef
2 tablespoons dry bread crumbs
1 tablespoon beaten egg
1½ teaspoon onion soup mix (dry)

Place margarine in custard cup. Microwave uncovered on high (100%) until melted, 30 to 45 seconds; stir in dill weed. Cut potato lengthwise into fourths. Brush cut sides with margarine mixture; arrange cut sides up on 9-inch plate. Wrap corn in microwavable paper towel; place on plate next to potato. Microwave uncovered on high (100%) until hot, 3 to 3½ minutes.

Mix ground beef, bread crumbs, egg and 1 teaspoon of the soup mix; shape into loaf. Place meat loaf on plate with corn and potato; sprinkle with remaining soup mix. Cover plate with microwavable paper towel and microwave until beef is no longer pink inside, 6 to 7 minutes.

Shrimp Kabob Dinner (page 40)

Pork Tenderloin Dinner

Cinnamon Sugar (below)
1 piece pork tenderloin (3 ounces)
⅛ teaspoon dried thyme
Dash of pepper
½ cup cauliflowerets
Snipped fresh chives
½ medium all-purpose apple, cored and cut into 4 wedges
1½ teaspoons apricot preserves

Prepare Cinnamon Sugar; reserve. Flatten pork tenderloin to ¼-inch thickness between plastic wrap or waxed paper; sprinkle with thyme and pepper. Roll up pork; place seam side down on 9-inch plate. Cover with vented plastic wrap and microwave on high (100%) until warm, 1 to 1½ minutes. Place cauliflower on plate next to pork; sprinkle with chives. Place apple on plate with pork and cauliflower; sprinkle with Cinnamon Sugar. Spoon preserves over pork. Cover with vented plastic wrap and microwave until pork is done and cauliflower is tender, 3 to 3½ minutes.

CINNAMON SUGAR

1¾ teaspoons sugar
¼ teaspoon ground cinnamon

Mix sugar and cinnamon.

Smoked Pork Chop Dinner

1 tablespoon margarine or butter
3 small new potatoes (about 2 ounces each)
1 cup shredded cabbage
3-ounce smoked, boneless pork chop
Dash of caraway seed
1 sprig parsley

Place margarine on 9-inch plate. Microwave uncovered on high (100%) until melted, 30 to 40 seconds. Pare a narrow strip around center of each potato. Coat potatoes with margarine; place on plate with margarine. Cover with vented plastic wrap and microwave until hot, 2 to 2½ minutes. Mix cabbage and margarine next to potatoes on plate. Place pork chop on cabbage; sprinkle with caraway seed. Cover with vented plastic wrap and microwave until pork is done and potatoes are tender, 4½ to 5 minutes. Garnish with parsley.

Rolled Chicken Breast Dinner

1 tablespoon margarine or butter
1 tablespoon cornflake crumbs
2 teaspoons grated Parmesan cheese
½ teaspoon parsley flakes
⅛ teaspoon paprika
1 boneless, skinless chicken breast half (3 ounces)
½ cup ¼-inch strips carrot
1 package (4½ ounces) frozen long grain white rice with peas and mushrooms

Place margarine on 9-inch plate. Microwave uncovered on high (100%) until melted, 30 to 40 seconds. Mix cornflake crumbs, cheese, parsley and paprika on waxed paper.

Flatten chicken breast half to ¼-inch thickness between plastic wrap or waxed paper. Coat chicken with crumb mixture. Dip into margarine; coat with remaining crumb mixture. Roll up chicken; place seam side down on plate. Mix carrot strips and margarine on plate. Remove plastic film from frozen tray of rice; place tray on plate next to carrots. Cover plate with vented plastic wrap and microwave until chicken is done, 6 to 7 minutes. Stir rice; empty onto plate.

Chicken Chunk Dinner

1 frozen hash brown potato patty
1 tablespoon sour cream
2 teaspoons milk
Dash of salt
Dash of pepper
¼ teaspoon parsley flakes
1 tablespoon margarine or butter
2 tablespoons Italian-style dry bread crumbs
⅛ teaspoon garlic salt
⅛ teaspoon paprika
1 boneless, skinless chicken breast half (about 3 ounces)
½ medium tomato
Dash of salt
Dash of pepper
1 teaspoon grated Parmesan cheese

Place potato patty on 9-inch plate. Cover with microwavable paper towel and microwave on high (100%) until hot, 2½ to 3 minutes; break up with fork. Stir in sour cream, milk, dash of salt and pepper. Mound potato mixture on plate; sprinkle with parsley.

Place margarine in custard cup. Microwave uncovered on high (100%) until melted, 30 to 45 seconds. Mix bread crumbs, garlic salt and paprika on waxed paper. Cut chicken breast half into 1-inch pieces. Dip chicken pieces into margarine; coat with crumb mixture. Arrange on plate next to potatoes. Place tomato, cut side up, on plate; sprinkle with dash of salt, pepper and the cheese. Cover with microwavable paper towel and microwave on high (100%) until chicken is done, 2½ to 3 minutes.

Turkey Parmesan Dinner

1 tablespoon margarine or butter
1 tablespoon Italian-style dry bread crumbs
1 tablespoon grated Parmesan cheese
¼ teaspoon paprika
1 slice uncooked turkey breast (about 2½ ounces)
1 cup broccoli flowerets
1 cup cooked long pasta
1 canned peach half
1 teaspoon currant jelly
Dash of Italian seasoning

Place margarine on 9-inch plate. Microwave uncovered on high (100%) until melted, 30 to 45 seconds. Mix bread crumbs, cheese and paprika on waxed paper. Coat turkey slice with crumb mixture. Dip into margarine; coat with remaining crumb mixture. Place turkey on plate with margarine. Mix broccoli and margarine on plate. Cover with vented plastic wrap and microwave until turkey is almost done, 3 to 3½ minutes. Place pasta on plate. Turn turkey over; place on pasta. Place peach half, cut side up, on plate with turkey and pasta; spoon jelly into center. Sprinkle turkey with Italian seasoning. Microwave uncovered until hot, 45 to 60 seconds.

Fish Fillet Dinner

3 small new potatoes (about 2 ounces each)
1 cup broccoli flowerets
1 teaspoon water
1 fresh or frozen (thawed) fish fillet (3½ ounces)
1 tablespoon margarine or butter
1 teaspoon lemon juice
⅛ teaspoon dried tarragon

Alternate potatoes and broccoli around edge of 9-inch plate; sprinkle with water. Cover with vented plastic wrap and microwave on high (100%) until hot, 2 to 2½ minutes. Place fish fillet in center of plate. Cover with vented plastic wrap and microwave until fish flakes easily with fork, 2½ to 3 minutes; drain. Place margarine, lemon juice and tarragon in small dish. Microwave uncovered on high (100%) until margarine is melted, 30 to 40 seconds; spoon over fish and vegetables.

Shrimp Kabob Dinner

1 package (4½ ounces) frozen long grain white rice with peas and mushrooms
4 ounces deveined and peeled medium raw shrimp (6 to 8)
6 chunks canned pineapple
4 cherry tomatoes
Four 1-inch pieces green pepper
1 tablespoon Italian dressing
1 dinner roll

Cut slit in center of plastic film on rice tray. Microwave tray of frozen rice on high (100%) until thawed, 2 to 2½ minutes; stir. Alternate shrimp, pineapple, tomatoes and green pepper on each of 2 wooden skewers. Place kabobs on 9-inch plate; brush with dressing. Place tray of rice mixture on plate next to kabobs. Microwave uncovered until shrimp are done, 2 to 2½ minutes. Empty rice onto plate with kabobs; place dinner roll on plate. Microwave uncovered until roll is warm, 30 to 40 seconds.

Turkey Parmesan Dinner

Mini-Meals

Frankfurter in Bun

1 SERVING

1 frankfurter
1 frankfurter bun

Place frankfurter in bun. Wrap in waxed paper; twist ends. Place on plate. Microwave on high (100%) until frankfurter is hot, 45 seconds to 1¼ minutes.

2 SERVINGS

2 frankfurters
2 frankfurter buns

Place frankfurters in buns. Wrap each in waxed paper; twist ends. Place on plate. Microwave on high (100%) until frankfurters are hot, 1 to 1½ minutes.

Beef Tacos

1 SERVING

¼ pound ground beef
2 tablespoons chopped onion
½ teaspoon finely chopped green chilies
⅛ teaspoon salt
Dash of ground cumin
½ small clove garlic, finely chopped
¼ cup chopped avocado
1 teaspoon lemon juice
¼ cup chopped tomato
2 taco shells
Sour cream
Shredded Cheddar cheese

Crumble ground beef into 2-cup measure. Cover loosely and microwave on high (100%) until very little pink remains, 1 to 1¼ minutes; break up and drain. Stir in onion, chilies, salt, cumin and garlic. Microwave uncovered until hot and onion is tender, 1 to 2 minutes.

Toss avocado and lemon juice; stir avocado and tomato into beef mixture. Spoon into taco shells. Top with sour cream and cheese. Serve with taco sauce if desired.

Beef Tacos

2 SERVINGS

½ pound ground beef
¼ cup chopped onion
1 teaspoon finely chopped green chilies
¼ teaspoon salt
Dash of ground cumin
1 small clove garlic, finely chopped
½ cup chopped avocado
2 teaspoons lemon juice
½ cup chopped tomato
4 taco shells
Sour cream
Shredded Cheddar cheese

Crumble ground beef into 4-cup measure. Cover loosely and microwave on high (100%) until very little pink remains, 1½ to 2 minutes; break up and drain. Stir in onion, chilies, salt, cumin and garlic. Microwave uncovered until hot and onion is tender, 2 to 3 minutes.

Toss avocado and lemon juice; stir avocado and tomato into beef mixture. Spoon into taco shells. Top with sour cream and cheese. Serve with taco sauce if desired.

Chili con Carne

1 SERVING

¼ pound ground beef

2 tablespoons finely chopped onion

1 teaspoon chili powder

⅛ teaspoon salt

Dash of ground red pepper

½ small clove garlic, finely chopped

1 can (7½ ounces) whole tomatoes, undrained

½ can (8-ounce size) kidney beans, undrained

Crumble ground beef into 16-ounce casserole. Cover loosely and microwave on high (100%) until very little pink remains, 1 to 1¼ minutes; break up and drain. Stir in remaining ingredients except beans; break up tomatoes. Cover loosely and microwave until onion is tender, 2 to 3 minutes. Stir in beans. Cover loosely and microwave until hot, 1½ to 2 minutes. Sprinkle with shredded Cheddar cheese and chopped green onions if desired.

2 SERVINGS

½ pound ground beef

¼ cup finely chopped onion

2 teaspoons chili powder

¼ teaspoon salt

Dash of ground red pepper

1 small clove garlic, finely chopped

1 can (14½ ounces) whole tomatoes, undrained

1 can (8 ounces) kidney beans, undrained

Crumble ground beef into 1-quart casserole. Cover loosely and microwave on high (100%) until very little pink remains, 1½ to 2 minutes; break up and drain. Stir in remaining ingredients except beans; break up tomatoes. Cover loosely and microwave until onion is tender, 4 to 5 minutes. Stir in beans. Cover loosely and microwave until hot, 2½ to 3 minutes. Sprinkle with shredded Cheddar cheese and chopped green onions if desired.

Burritos

1 SERVING

¼ pound bulk pork sausage

¼ cup jalapeño bean dip

1 tablespoon taco sauce

¼ to ½ teaspoon chili powder

½ small clove garlic, finely chopped

Dash of salt

Two 6-inch flour tortillas

¼ cup shredded Cheddar cheese

Crumble pork sausage into 2-cup measure. Cover loosely and microwave on high (100%) until very little pink remains, 1½ to 2 minutes; break up

2 SERVINGS

½ pound bulk pork sausage

½ cup jalapeño bean dip

2 tablespoons taco sauce

½ to 1 teaspoon chili powder

1 small clove garlic, finely chopped

⅛ teaspoon salt

Four 6-inch flour tortillas

½ cup shredded Cheddar cheese

Crumble pork sausage into 4-cup measure. Cover loosely and microwave on high (100%) until very little pink remains, 2 to 2½ minutes; break up and drain. Stir in bean dip, taco sauce, chili powder, garlic and salt. Cover loosely and microwave until hot and bubbly, 1¼ to 2 minutes; stir. Cover to keep warm.

Wrap tortillas in damp cloth and microwave on high (100%) until softened, 30 to 45 seconds. Spread about ⅓ cup filling on each tortilla (keep remaining tortilla covered to prevent it from drying out); sprinkle with 2 tablespoons cheese. Fold up bottom of tortilla. Fold sides over and roll from bottom. Arrange burritos, seam sides down, on dinner plate. Cover loosely and microwave on high (100%) until hot, 1¼ to 2 minutes. Serve with taco sauce if desired.

and drain. Stir in bean dip, taco sauce, chili powder, garlic and salt. Cover loosely and microwave until hot and bubbly, 2 to 3½ minutes; stir. Cover to keep warm.

Wrap tortillas in damp cloth and microwave on high (100%) until softened, 1 to 2 minutes. Spread about ⅓ cup filling on each tortilla (keep remaining tortillas covered to prevent them from drying out); sprinkle with 2 tablespoons cheese. Fold up bottom of tortilla. Fold sides over and roll from bottom. Arrange burritos, seam sides down, forming a square on plate. Cover loosely and microwave on high (100%) until hot, 2½ to 3½ minutes. Serve with taco sauce if desired.

Tortilla Roll-up

1 SERVING

1½ teaspoons margarine or butter
Dash of poppy seed
⅛ teaspoon prepared mustard
One 8-inch flour tortilla
½ package (2½-ounce size) smoked sliced ham
¼ cup shredded Swiss cheese

Place margarine, poppy seed and mustard in 6-ounce custard cup. Microwave uncovered on high (100%) until margarine is melted, 20 to 30 seconds; stir until margarine is smooth. Spread on tortilla. Place ham on tortilla; sprinkle with cheese. Roll tortilla around ham. Wrap in microwavable paper towel. Microwave on high (100%) until hot, 30 to 40 seconds.

2 SERVINGS

1 tablespoon margarine or butter
⅛ teaspoon poppy seed
¼ teaspoon prepared mustard
Two 8-inch flour tortillas
1 package (2½ ounces) smoked sliced ham
½ cup shredded Swiss cheese

Place margarine, poppy seed and mustard in 6-ounce custard cup. Microwave uncovered on high (100%) until margarine is melted, 30 to 45 seconds; stir until margarine is smooth. Spread on tortillas. Place ham on tortillas; sprinkle with cheese. Roll tortillas around ham. Wrap each tortilla in microwavable paper towel. Microwave on high (100%) until hot, 1 to 1¼ minutes.

Chicken Salad Croissant

1 SERVING

1 boneless, skinless chicken breast half (about 3 ounces)
2 tablespoons creamy ranch-style dressing
¼ teaspoon prepared mustard
2 tablespoons chopped cucumber
2 tablespoons chopped tomato
1 tablespoon chopped cashews
1 croissant
Margarine, butter, mayonnaise or salad dressing
¼ cup alfalfa sprouts

Place chicken breast half in 16-ounce casserole or on plate. Cover tightly and microwave on high (100%) until thickest part is done, 2 to 3 minutes. Uncover and refrigerate until cool enough to handle, about 10 minutes.

Cut chicken into ¼-inch pieces. Place chicken, dressing, mustard, cucumber, tomato and cashews in bowl; toss. Cover and refrigerate until chilled. Just before serving, cut croissant horizontally into halves; spread with margarine. Spread chicken mixture over bottom of croissant; top with alfalfa sprouts and the other croissant half.

2 SERVINGS

2 boneless, skinless chicken breast halves (about 3 ounces each)
¼ cup creamy ranch-style dressing
½ teaspoon prepared mustard
¼ cup chopped cucumber
¼ cup chopped tomato
2 tablespoons chopped cashews
2 croissants, cut lengthwise into halves
Margarine, butter, mayonnaise or salad dressing
½ cup alfalfa sprouts

Place chicken breast halves in 16-ounce casserole or on plate with thickest parts toward outside edges. Cover tightly and microwave on high (100%) until thickest parts are done, 3 to 4 minutes. Uncover and refrigerate until cool enough to handle, about 10 minutes.

Cut chicken into ¼-inch pieces. Place chicken, dressing, mustard, cucumber, tomato and cashews in bowl; toss. Cover and refrigerate until chilled. Just before serving, spread cut sides of croissant halves with margarine. Spread chicken mixture over bottoms of croissants; top with alfalfa sprouts and the other croissant halves.

Chicken Salad Croissant

Veggie Pita Pizza

1 SERVING

1 pita bread (6 inches in diameter)
1 to 2 tablespoons pizza sauce or spaghetti
  sauce
½ cup chopped zucchini
1 tablespoon chopped onion
¼ cup chopped tomato
1 tablespoon sliced ripe olives
⅛ teaspoon salt
Dash of dried basil
2 tablespoons shredded mozzarella cheese

Split pita bread horizontally into halves. Reserve half for another use.

Spread pizza sauce on pita half; place on small plate. Place zucchini and onion in 10-ounce casserole. Microwave uncovered on high (100%) until tender, 1½ to 2 minutes. Stir in tomato, olives, salt and basil. Spoon vegetables onto pita half; top with cheese. Microwave uncovered on high (100%) until hot, 30 to 45 seconds. Cut into wedges.

2 SERVINGS

1 pita bread (6 inches in diameter), split
  horizontally into halves
2 to 4 tablespoons pizza sauce or spaghetti
  sauce
1 cup chopped zucchini
2 tablespoons chopped onion
½ cup chopped tomato
2 tablespoons sliced ripe olives
¼ teaspoon salt
⅛ teaspoon dried basil
¼ cup shredded mozzarella cheese

Spread pizza sauce on pita halves; place on small plates. Place zucchini and onion in 2-cup casserole. Microwave uncovered on high (100%) until tender, 2½ to 3 minutes. Stir in tomato, olives, salt and basil. Spoon vegetables onto pita halves; top with cheese. Microwave uncovered on high (100%) until hot, 45 to 60 seconds. Cut into wedges.

Veggie Pita Pizza

Blue Cheese Burger

1 SERVING

¼ pound ground beef
1 tablespoon blue cheese, crumbled
⅛ teaspoon onion powder
⅛ teaspoon salt
Dash of pepper
1 English muffin, split and toasted
1 tablespoon blue cheese dressing
1 pimiento-stuffed olive, sliced

Mix ground beef, cheese, onion powder, salt and pepper. Shape into patty, about ¾ inch thick. Place on rack in dish. Cover with waxed paper and microwave on high (100%) until almost done, 2 to 3 minutes. Place on bottom of English muffin. Top with dressing, olive and top of English muffin.

2 SERVINGS

½ pound ground beef
2 tablespoons blue cheese, crumbled
¼ teaspoon onion powder
¼ teaspoon salt
⅛ teaspoon pepper
2 English muffins, split and toasted
2 tablespoons blue cheese dressing
2 pimiento-stuffed olives, sliced

Mix ground beef, cheese, onion powder, salt and pepper. Shape into 2 patties, about ¾ inch thick. Place on rack in dish. Cover with waxed paper and microwave on high (100%) until almost done, 3 to 4 minutes. Place on bottoms of English muffins. Top with dressing, olives and tops of English muffins.

Steak Burger

1 SERVING

¼ pound ground beef
1 teaspoon steak sauce
½ teaspoon Dijon-style mustard
⅛ teaspoon onion powder
Dash of salt
Dash of pepper
2 mushrooms, sliced
1 hard roll, split and toasted

Mix ground beef, steak sauce, mustard, onion powder, salt and pepper. Shape into patty, about ¾ inch thick. Arrange mushrooms in circle on rack in 11 × 7 × 1½-inch dish; place patty on mushrooms. Cover with waxed paper and microwave on high (100%) until almost done, 2 to 3 minutes. Serve on hard roll with mushrooms on top.

2 SERVINGS

½ pound ground beef
2 teaspoons steak sauce
1 teaspoon Dijon-style mustard
¼ teaspoon onion powder
⅛ teaspoon salt
⅛ teaspoon pepper
4 mushrooms, sliced
2 hard rolls, split and toasted

Mix ground beef, steak sauce, mustard, onion powder, salt and pepper. Shape into 2 patties, about ¾ inch thick. Arrange mushrooms in 2 circles on rack in 11 × 7 × 1½-inch dish; place patties on mushrooms. Cover with waxed paper and microwave on high (100%) until almost done, 3 to 4 minutes. Serve on hard rolls with mushrooms on top.

Chicken Soup

1 SERVING

¼ cup sliced mushrooms

2 tablespoons sliced celery

2 tablespoons sliced carrot

1½ teaspoons margarine or butter

1 boneless, skinless chicken breast half (about 3 ounces)

2 tablespoons uncooked instant rice

1 cup hot water

1 teaspoon instant chicken bouillon (dry)

Dash of dried thyme

Place mushrooms, celery, carrot and margarine in 16-ounce casserole. Cover tightly and microwave on high (100%) until vegetables are tender, 1½ to 2 minutes. Cut chicken breast half into ¼-inch strips. Stir chicken and remaining ingredients into vegetable mixture. Cover tightly and microwave until boiling, 2½ to 3 minutes.

2 SERVINGS

½ cup sliced mushrooms

¼ cup sliced celery

¼ cup sliced carrot

1 tablespoon margarine or butter

2 boneless, skinless chicken breast halves (about 3 ounces each)

¼ cup uncooked instant rice

2 cups hot water

2 teaspoons instant chicken bouillon (dry)

⅛ teaspoon dried thyme

Place mushrooms, celery, carrot and margarine in 1-quart casserole. Cover tightly and microwave on high (100%) until vegetables are tender, 2½ to 3 minutes. Cut chicken breast half into ¼-inch strips. Stir chicken and remaining ingredients into vegetable mixture. Cover tightly and microwave until boiling, 5 to 6 minutes.

Zucchini Soup

1 SERVING

1 slice bacon, cut into ½-inch pieces

¾ cup milk

¼ cup hot water

1½ teaspoons finely chopped onion

1 teaspoon instant chicken bouillon (dry)

4 drops red pepper sauce

¼ cup shredded zucchini

Place bacon in 2-cup measure. Cover loosely and microwave on high (100%) until almost crisp, 1½ to 2 minutes. Remove bacon with slotted spoon; crumble and reserve. Stir remaining ingredients except zucchini into bacon fat. Cover tightly and microwave until boiling, 1½ to 2 minutes. Stir in zucchini. Microwave uncovered until hot, 30 to 60 seconds. Sprinkle with bacon.

2 SERVINGS

2 slices bacon, cut into ½-inch pieces

1½ cups milk

½ cup hot water

1 tablespoon finely chopped onion

2 teaspoons instant chicken bouillon (dry)

8 drops red pepper sauce

½ cup shredded zucchini

Place bacon in 4-cup measure. Cover loosely and microwave on high (100%) until almost crisp, 2½ to 3 minutes. Remove bacon with slotted spoon; crumble and reserve. Stir remaining ingredients except zucchini into bacon fat. Cover tightly and microwave until boiling, 2 to 2½ minutes. Stir in zucchini. Microwave uncovered until hot, 1 to 1½ minutes. Sprinkle with bacon.

Cheese Soup

1 SERVING

2 tablespoons water
1 tablespoon finely chopped celery
1 teaspoon finely chopped onion
1 tablespoon margarine or butter
1 tablespoon all-purpose flour
¾ cup milk
1 teaspoon instant chicken bouillon (dry)
⅛ teaspoon paprika
¼ cup shredded sharp process American cheese

Place water, celery and onion in 1-cup measure. Cover tightly and microwave on high (100%) until vegetables are tender, 1 to 1½ minutes; reserve.

Place margarine in 2-cup measure. Microwave uncovered on high (100%) until melted, 20 to 30 seconds. Mix in flour. Stir in celery and onion, milk, bouillon and paprika. Microwave uncovered until boiling, 1½ to 2 minutes. Stir in cheese. Microwave uncovered on medium-high (70%) until melted, 1 to 1½ minutes; stir. Garnish with popcorn or croutons if desired.

2 SERVINGS

¼ cup water
2 tablespoons finely chopped celery
2 teaspoons finely chopped onion
2 tablespoons margarine or butter
2 tablespoons all-purpose flour
1½ cups milk
2 teaspoons instant chicken bouillon (dry)
¼ teaspoon paprika
½ cup shredded sharp process American cheese

Place water, celery and onion in 1-cup measure. Cover tightly and microwave on high (100%) until tender, 1½ to 2 minutes; reserve.

Place margarine in 4-cup measure. Microwave uncovered on high (100%) until melted, 45 to 60 seconds. Mix in flour. Stir in celery and onion, milk, bouillon and paprika. Microwave uncovered until boiling, 2½ to 3½ minutes. Stir in cheese. Microwave uncovered on medium-high (70%) until melted, 1½ to 2 minutes; stir. Garnish with popcorn or croutons if desired.

Fresh Mushroom Soup

1 SERVING

1 tablespoon chopped green onion (with top)
1½ teaspoons margarine or butter
1½ teaspoons all-purpose flour
¾ cup hot water
½ cup sliced mushrooms
1 teaspoon instant chicken bouillon (dry)
Dash of white pepper
¼ cup half-and-half

2 SERVINGS

2 tablespoons chopped green onion (with top)
1 tablespoon margarine or butter
1 tablespoon all-purpose flour
1½ cups hot water
1 cup sliced mushrooms
2 teaspoons instant chicken bouillon (dry)
Dash of white pepper
½ cup half-and-half

Place onion and margarine in 2-cup measure. Cover tightly and microwave on high (100%) until onion is tender, 1 to 1½ minutes. Mix in flour. Stir in water, mushrooms, bouillon and white pepper. Cover tightly and microwave until boiling, 1½ to 2 minutes. Stir in half-and-half. Microwave uncovered until hot, 30 to 60 seconds.

Place onion and margarine in 4-cup measure. Cover tightly and microwave on high (100%) until onion is tender, 1½ to 2 minutes. Mix in flour. Stir in water, mushrooms, bouillon and white pepper. Cover tightly and microwave until boiling, 2 to 2½ minutes. Stir in half-and-half. Microwave uncovered until hot, 1 to 1½ minutes.

Fiesta Salad

1 SERVING

One 8-inch flour tortilla
¼ pound ground beef
2 tablespoons picante sauce
1 cup shredded lettuce
¼ cup chopped tomato
1 tablespoon shredded Cheddar cheese
1 tablespoon sour cream

Gently press tortilla into 16-ounce round casserole, allowing edge to extend above casserole. Microwave uncovered on high (100%) until edge is light brown, 1½ to 2 minutes. Carefully remove tortilla shell; cool.

Crumble ground beef into 16-ounce casserole. Microwave uncovered on high (100%) 1 minute; stir. Microwave uncovered until very little pink remains, 45 to 60 seconds longer; break up and drain. Stir in picante sauce. Layer lettuce and tomato in tortilla shell on plate. Spoon beef mixture over tomato. Top salad with cheese and sour cream.

2 SERVINGS

Two 8-inch flour tortillas
½ pound ground beef
¼ cup picante sauce
2 cups shredded lettuce
½ cup chopped tomato
2 tablespoons shredded Cheddar cheese
2 tablespoons sour cream

Gently press tortillas into two 16-ounce round casseroles, allowing edges to extend above casseroles. Microwave uncovered on high (100%) until edges are light brown, 3 to 3½ minutes. Carefully remove tortilla shells; cool.

Crumble ground beef into 24-ounce casserole. Microwave uncovered on high (100%) 2 minutes; stir. Microwave uncovered until very little pink remains, 1 to 1½ minutes longer; break up and drain. Stir in picante sauce. Layer lettuce and tomato in tortilla shells on plates. Spoon beef mixture over tomato. Top salad with cheese and sour cream.

Chicken-Pasta Salad

1 SERVING

1 boneless, skinless chicken breast half (about 3 ounces)
¼ cup uncooked rotini or other small pasta
¼ cup chopped tomato
¼ cup chopped cucumber
1 small green onion, thinly sliced
2 tablespoons mayonnaise or salad dressing
⅛ teaspoon salt
Dash of dried dill weed

Place chicken breast half in 16-ounce casserole or on plate. Cover tightly and microwave on high (100%) until thickest part is done, 2 to 3 minutes. Uncover and refrigerate until cool enough to handle, about 10 minutes.

Cook rotini as directed on package; drain. Rinse in cold water; drain. Cut chicken into cubes. Mix chicken, rotini and remaining ingredients in bowl. Cover and refrigerate until chilled, about 2 hours.

2 SERVINGS

2 boneless, skinless chicken breast halves (about 3 ounces each)
½ cup uncooked rotini or other small pasta
½ cup chopped tomato
½ cup chopped cucumber
1 medium green onion, thinly sliced
¼ cup mayonnaise or salad dressing
¼ teaspoon salt
⅛ teaspoon dried dill weed

Place chicken breast halves in 16-ounce casserole or on plate with thickest parts to outside edges. Cover tightly and microwave on high (100%) until thickest parts are done, 3 to 4 minutes. Uncover and refrigerate until cool enough to handle, about 10 minutes.

Cook rotini as directed on package; drain. Rinse in cold water; drain. Cut chicken into cubes. Mix chicken, rotini and remaining ingredients in bowl. Cover and refrigerate until chilled, about 3 hours.

Spicy Guacamole Dip

1 SERVING

Prepare Spicy Guacamole Dip for 2 Servings. Cover and refrigerate remaining dip for another meal. To reheat, if desired, microwave uncovered on high (100%) until warm, 20 to 30 seconds.

2 SERVINGS

1 tablespoon chopped onion
1 small clove garlic, finely chopped
1 teaspoon margarine or butter
1 small ripe avocado, peeled
1 teaspoon lemon juice
3 tablespoons picante sauce
Vegetables, chips or crackers

Place onion, garlic and margarine in 16-ounce casserole. Microwave uncovered on high (100%) until onion is tender, 1 to 1¼ minutes. Cut avocado lengthwise into halves; remove pit. Place avocado in small bowl; mash with fork until smooth. Stir avocado, lemon juice and picante sauce into onion mixture. Serve warm or chilled with vegetables.

Maple-Nut Cheese Spread

1 SERVING

Prepare Maple-Nut Cheese Spread for 2 Servings; serve with 1 small apple or pear. Cover and refrigerate remaining cheese spread for another meal.

2 SERVINGS

½ package (3-ounce size) cream cheese
2 teaspoons maple-flavored syrup
1 tablespoon chopped walnuts
1 drop maple flavoring
1 medium apple or pear

Place cream cheese in small bowl. Microwave uncovered on high (100%) until softened, 30 to 40 seconds. Stir in remaining ingredients except apple. Core and slice apple; arrange on plate. Serve with spread.

Pizza Potato Snacks

1 SERVING

1 medium potato
1 tablespoon pizza sauce or spaghetti sauce
2 tablespoons shredded mozzarella cheese

Prick potato once with fork to allow steam to escape. Microwave uncovered on high (100%) 1½ minutes; turn potato over. Microwave uncovered until tender, 1½ to 2 minutes longer; cool slightly.

Cut potato crosswise into ½-inch slices. Place on plate. Top with pizza sauce and cheese. Microwave uncovered on high (100%) until cheese is melted, 30 to 45 seconds.

CHEDDAR 'N BACON POTATO SNACKS. Omit pizza sauce. Substitute Cheddar cheese for the mozzarella cheese; sprinkle with crumbled cooked bacon or imitation bacon pieces.

2 SERVINGS

1 large potato
2 tablespoons pizza sauce or spaghetti sauce
¼ cup shredded mozzarella cheese

Prick potato once with fork to allow steam to escape. Microwave uncovered on high (100%) 2½ minutes; turn potato over. Microwave uncovered until tender, 2 to 2½ minutes longer; cool slightly.

Cut potato crosswise into ½-inch slices. Place on plate. Top with pizza sauce and cheese. Microwave uncovered on high (100%) until cheese is melted, 45 to 60 seconds.

PICANTE POTATO SNACKS. Substitute picante sauce for the pizza sauce and Monterey Jack cheese for the mozzarella cheese.

Peppy Cheese Chips

1 SERVING

¼ cup shredded Cheddar cheese
1½ teaspoons picante sauce or taco sauce
1½ teaspoons chopped green olives
2 tablespoons chopped tomato
8 tostada chips

Mix cheese, picante sauce, olives and tomato. Arrange chips in single layer on 6-inch plate. Spoon mixture evenly over chips. Microwave uncovered on high (100%) until cheese is melted, 30 to 45 seconds.

2 SERVINGS

½ cup shredded Cheddar cheese
1 tablespoon picante sauce or taco sauce
1 tablespoon chopped green olives
¼ cup chopped tomato
16 tostada chips

Mix cheese, picante sauce, olives and tomato. Arrange chips in single layer on 8-inch plate. Spoon mixture evenly over chips. Microwave uncovered on high (100%) until cheese is melted, 45 to 60 seconds.

Peppy Cheese Chips

Honey-Lime Fruit Salad

1 SERVING

Honey-Lime Dressing (below)
1 cup cut-up fresh fruit (apples, oranges, grapes, bananas or pears)

Prepare Honey-Lime Dressing; cool slightly. Pour half over fruit in bowl; toss until fruit is glazed. Cover and refrigerate remaining dressing for another meal.

2 SERVINGS

Honey-Lime Dressing (below)
2 cups cut-up fresh fruit (apples, oranges, grapes, bananas or pears)

Prepare Honey-Lime Dressing; cool slightly. Pour over fruit in bowl; toss until fruit is glazed.

HONEY-LIME DRESSING

1 tablespoon lime juice
1 tablespoon honey
½ teaspoon cornstarch
⅛ teaspoon poppy seed

Mix lime juice, honey, cornstarch and poppy seed in 1-cup measure. Microwave uncovered on high (100%) until mixture thickens and boils, 30 to 40 seconds.

Raspberry Yogurt Salad

1 SERVING

⅓ cup hot water
1 tablespoon plus 1 teaspoon raspberry-flavored gelatin (dry)
⅓ cup raspberry yogurt

Place hot water in 2-cup measure. Microwave uncovered on high (100%) until boiling, 1 to 1½ minutes. Stir in gelatin until dissolved. Mix in yogurt. Pour into 6-ounce custard cup. Refrigerate until set, about 2 hours.

2 SERVINGS

¾ cup hot water
3 tablespoons raspberry-flavored gelatin (½ three-ounce package)
1 container (6 ounces) raspberry yogurt

Place hot water in 2-cup measure. Microwave uncovered on high (100%) until boiling, 1½ to 2 minutes. Stir in gelatin until dissolved. Mix in yogurt. Pour into 2 six-ounce custard cups. Refrigerate until set, about 2 hours.

Honey-Lime Fruit Salad

Garlic-Basil Burger

1 SERVING

¼ pound ground beef
1 tablespoon dry bread crumbs
1 tablespoon chopped green onion
  (with top)
½ teaspoon lemon juice
⅛ teaspoon salt
Dash of pepper
½ teaspoon snipped fresh or dash of dried
  basil
½ small clove garlic, finely chopped
1 slice bacon, cut into halves

Mix all ingredients except bacon. Shape into patty, about ¾ inch thick. Place on rack in dish. Cover with waxed paper and microwave on high (100%) until almost done, 2 to 3¼ minutes. Remove from rack; let stand 3 minutes.

Place bacon on rack in same dish. Cover loosely and microwave on high (100%) until almost crisp, 1¼ to 1½ minutes; drain. Crisscross half slices of bacon on patty.

2 SERVINGS

½ pound ground beef
2 tablespoons dry bread crumbs
2 tablespoons chopped green onion
  (with top)
1 teaspoon lemon juice
¼ teaspoon salt
Dash of pepper
1 teaspoon snipped fresh or dash of dried
  basil
1 small clove garlic, finely chopped
2 slices bacon, cut into halves

Mix all ingredients except bacon. Shape into 2 patties, about ¾ inch thick. Place on rack in dish. Cover with waxed paper and microwave on high (100%) until almost done, 2¾ to 4 minutes. Remove from rack; let stand 3 minutes.

Place bacon on rack in same dish. Cover loosely and microwave on high (100%) until almost crisp, 1½ to 2½ minutes; drain. Crisscross half slices of bacon on patties.

Garlic-Basil Burger

Spaghetti with Meat Sauce

1 SERVING

¼ pound ground beef

½ cup tomato sauce

2 tablespoons dry red wine

1 tablespoon chopped onion

1 tablespoon finely chopped green pepper

⅛ teaspoon salt

Dash of pepper

Dash of dried basil

1 small clove garlic, crushed

2 mushrooms, thinly sliced

1 cup hot cooked spaghetti

Crumble ground beef into 2-cup measure. Cover loosely and microwave on high (100%) until very little pink remains, 1 to 1¼ minutes; break up and drain. Stir in remaining ingredients except spaghetti. Cover loosely and microwave 1 minute; stir. Cover loosely and microwave until bubbly and mushrooms are tender, 1½ to 2 minutes longer. Pour over hot spaghetti. Serve with grated Parmesan cheese if desired.

2 SERVINGS

½ pound ground beef

1 cup tomato sauce

3 tablespoons dry red wine

2 tablespoons chopped onion

2 tablespoons finely chopped green pepper

¼ teaspoon salt

Dash of pepper

Dash of dried basil

1 large clove garlic, crushed

4 mushrooms, thinly sliced

2 cups hot cooked spaghetti

Crumble ground beef into 4-cup measure. Cover loosely and microwave on high (100%) until very little pink remains, 1½ to 2 minutes; break up and drain. Stir in remaining ingredients except spaghetti. Cover loosely and microwave 2 minutes; stir. Cover loosely and microwave until bubbly and mushrooms are tender, 1½ to 2 minutes longer. Pour over hot spaghetti. Serve with grated Parmesan cheese if desired.

Hot Ham Salad

1 SERVING

2 thin slices (1 ounce each) ham, cut into
  ½-inch pieces

¼ cup herb-seasoned croutons

¼ cup thinly sliced celery

¼ cup frozen green peas, thawed

¼ cup mayonnaise or salad dressing

¼ teaspoon instant minced onion

Dash of pepper

1 tablespoon shredded Cheddar cheese

2 SERVINGS

4 thin slices (1 ounce each) ham, cut into
  ½-inch pieces

½ cup herb-seasoned croutons

½ cup thinly sliced celery

½ cup frozen green peas, thawed

½ cup mayonnaise or salad dressing

½ teaspoon instant minced onion

⅛ teaspoon pepper

2 tablespoons shredded Cheddar cheese

Mix all ingredients except cheese. Spoon lightly into 14-ounce ramekin or shallow casserole. Sprinkle with cheese. Cover loosely and microwave on medium-high (70%) until hot and bubbly, 2½ to 3½ minutes.

Mix all ingredients except cheese. Spoon lightly into two 14-ounce ramekins or shallow casseroles. Sprinkle with cheese. Cover loosely and microwave on medium-high (70%) until hot and bubbly, 3½ to 4½ minutes.

Lemon-Honey Pork Chop

1 SERVING

4-ounce pork loin chop (½ inch thick)
⅛ teaspoon salt
Dash of pepper
1 tablespoon water
1 tablespoon honey
⅛ teaspoon grated lemon peel
1½ teaspoons lemon juice
¼ teaspoon parsley flakes
½ small clove garlic, finely chopped
½ teaspoon cornstarch
1½ teaspoons cold water
1 thin slice lemon

Place pork chop in 22-ounce shallow casserole. Sprinkle with salt and pepper. Mix 1 tablespoon water, the honey, lemon peel, lemon juice, parsley and garlic; pour over pork. Cover with vented plastic wrap and microwave on medium (50%) 3 minutes; rotate casserole ¼ turn. Microwave, rotating casserole ¼ turn every 3 minutes, until pork is done, 4 to 7 minutes longer. Remove pork to warm plate.

Mix cornstarch and 1½ teaspoons water; stir into mixture in casserole. Cover tightly and microwave until mixture thickens and boils, 30 to 60 seconds. Spoon sauce over pork. Garnish with lemon slice and serve with hot cooked wild or white rice if desired.

2 SERVINGS

Two 4-ounce pork loin chops (½ inch thick)
¼ teaspoon salt
⅛ teaspoon pepper
2 tablespoons water
2 tablespoons honey
¼ teaspoon grated lemon peel
1 tablespoon lemon juice
½ teaspoon parsley flakes
1 small clove garlic, finely chopped
1 teaspoon cornstarch
1 tablespoon cold water
2 thin slices lemon

Place pork chops in 8 × 8 × 2-inch dish, with thickest parts to outside edges. Sprinkle with salt and pepper. Mix 2 tablespoons water, the honey, lemon peel, lemon juice, parsley and garlic; pour over pork. Cover with vented plastic wrap and microwave on medium (50%) 5 minutes; rotate dish ¼ turn. Microwave, rotating casserole ¼ turn every 3 minutes, until pork is done, 12 to 15 minutes longer. Remove pork to warm plates.

Mix cornstarch and 1 tablespoon water; stir into mixture in dish. Cover tightly and microwave until mixture thickens and boils, 1 to 2 minutes. Spoon sauce over pork. Garnish with lemon slices and serve with hot cooked wild or white rice if desired.

Currant-glazed Pork Chop

1 SERVING

2 tablespoons red currant jelly
2 tablespoons chili sauce
Dash of ground allspice
1 smoked pork chop (½ inch thick)

Mix jelly, chili sauce and allspice in 1-cup measure. Cover with waxed paper and microwave on high (100%) until jelly is melted, 30 to 45 seconds.

Place pork chop in 16-ounce shallow casserole. Spread half of the jelly mixture over pork. Cover with waxed paper and microwave on high (100%) 1 minute. Turn pork over and spread with remaining jelly mixture; rotate casserole ¼ turn. Cover with waxed paper and microwave until pork is done, 2½ to 3½ minutes longer.

2 SERVINGS

¼ cup red currant jelly
¼ cup chili sauce
⅛ teaspoon ground allspice
2 smoked pork chops (½ inch thick)

Mix jelly, chili sauce and allspice in 1-cup measure. Cover with waxed paper and microwave on high (100%) until jelly is melted, 1 to 1½ minutes.

Place pork chops in 8 × 8 × 2-inch dish, with thickest parts toward outside edges. Spread half of the jelly mixture over pork. Cover with waxed paper and microwave on high (100%) 2 minutes. Turn pork over and spread with remaining jelly mixture; rotate dish ¼ turn. Cover with waxed paper and microwave until pork is done, 4 to 6 minutes longer.

Fruited Pork

1 SERVING

4 ounces pork boneless shoulder, cut into
  ½-inch pieces (½ cup)
2 tablespoons chopped onion
¼ cup chopped apple
2 tablespoons water
1 teaspoon all-purpose flour
½ teaspoon instant chicken bouillon (dry)
Dash of salt
½ can (8-ounce size) sauerkraut, drained
4 dried apricots or prunes, cut up
¾ cup hot cooked spaetzle or noodles
Snipped parsley

2 SERVINGS

8 ounces pork boneless shoulder, cut into
  ½-inch pieces (1 cup)
¼ cup chopped onion
½ cup chopped apple
¼ cup water
2 teaspoons all-purpose floor
1 teaspoon instant chicken bouillon (dry)
⅛ teaspoon salt
1 can (8 ounces) sauerkraut, drained
8 dried apricots or prunes, cut up
1½ cups hot cooked spaetzle or noodles
Snipped parsley

Mix pork and onion in 16-ounce casserole. Cover with vented plastic wrap and microwave on medium (50%), stirring every 3 minutes, until pork is tender, 5 to 7 minutes. Stir in remaining ingredients except spaetzle and parsley. Cover with vented plastic wrap and microwave, stirring every 3 minutes, until hot and thickened, 3 to 4 minutes. Serve with hot spaetzle; sprinkle with parsley.

Mix pork and onion in 1-quart casserole. Cover with vented plastic wrap and microwave on medium (50%), stirring every 3 minutes, until pork is tender, 9 to 12 minutes. Stir in remaining ingredients except spaetzle and parsley. Cover with vented plastic wrap and microwave, stirring every 3 minutes, until hot and thickened, 5 to 7 minutes. Serve with hot spaetzle; sprinkle with parsley.

Pork Tenderloin with Mustard Sauce

1 SERVING

1 piece pork tenderloin (4 ounces)
⅛ teaspoon salt
2 tablespoons chopped onion
2 tablespoons chopped green pepper
2 tablespoons water
2 teaspoons Dijon-style mustard
½ teaspoon all-purpose flour

Place pork tenderloin in 16-ounce shallow casserole. Sprinkle with salt and onion. Cover with vented plastic wrap and microwave on medium (50%) 2 minutes; rotate casserole ¼ turn. Microwave 2 minutes longer. Mix remaining ingredients; spoon over pork. Cover with vented plastic wrap and microwave, rotating casserole ¼ turn every 3 minutes, until pork is done, 2 to 4 minutes.

2 SERVINGS

2 pieces pork tenderloin (4 ounces each)
¼ teaspoon salt
¼ cup chopped onion
¼ cup chopped green pepper
¼ cup water
1 tablespoon plus 1 teaspoon Dijon-style mustard
1 teaspoon all-purpose flour

Place pork tenderloin in 24-ounce shallow casserole. Sprinkle with salt and onion. Cover with vented plastic wrap and microwave on medium (50%) 4 minutes; rotate casserole ¼ turn. Microwave 4 minutes longer. Mix remaining ingredients; spoon over pork. Cover with vented plastic wrap and microwave, rotating casserole ¼ turn every 3 minutes, until pork is done, 4 to 6 minutes.

Sweet-and-Sour Pork

1 SERVING

3 ounces pork tenderloin, cut into ½-inch pieces

1 teaspoon margarine or butter

½ can (8¼-ounce size) pineapple chunks in syrup, drained (reserve ¼ cup syrup)

1 teaspoon cornstarch

2 tablespoons catsup

1 teaspoon sugar

1 teaspoon soy sauce

4 drops red pepper sauce

¼ medium green pepper, cut into ⅛-inch-thick strips

3 cherry tomatoes, cut into halves

¾ cup hot cooked rice

Mix pork and margarine in 16-ounce casserole. Cover tightly and microwave on medium (50%), stirring every 2 minutes, until pork is no longer pink, 2 to 3 minutes. Add enough water to reserved pineapple syrup to measure ⅓ cup; stir in cornstarch. Stir syrup mixture, catsup, sugar, soy sauce and pepper sauce into pork mixture. Cover tightly and microwave, stirring every 2 minutes, until mixture thickens and boils and pork is done, 4 to 5 minutes. Cut pineapple chunks into halves. Stir pineapple, green pepper and tomatoes into pork mixture. Cover tightly and microwave until hot, 1 to 2 minutes. Serve over hot rice.

2 SERVINGS

6 ounces pork tenderloin, cut into ½-inch pieces

2 teaspoons margarine or butter

1 can (8¼ ounces) pineapple chunks in syrup, drained (reserve ½ cup syrup)

2 teaspoons cornstarch

¼ cup catsup

2 teaspoons sugar

2 teaspoons soy sauce

⅛ teaspoon red pepper sauce

½ medium green pepper, cut into ⅛-inch-thick strips

6 cherry tomatoes, cut into halves

1½ cups hot cooked rice

Mix pork and margarine in 1-quart casserole. Cover tightly and microwave on medium (50%), stirring every 2 minutes, until pork is no longer pink, 4 to 6 minutes. Add enough water to reserved pineapple syrup to measure ⅔ cup; stir in cornstarch. Stir syrup mixture, catsup, sugar, soy sauce and pepper sauce into pork mixture. Cover tightly and microwave, stirring every 2 minutes, until mixture thickens and boils and pork is done, 6 to 8 minutes. Cut pineapple chunks into halves. Stir pineapple, green pepper and tomatoes into pork mixture. Cover tightly and microwave until hot, 2 to 3 minutes. Serve over hot rice.

Sausage-filled Tortillas

1 SERVING

2 ounces bulk pork sausage

2 tablespoons coarsely chopped tomato

1 teaspoon chili powder

1 teaspoon lemon juice

Dash of salt

½ small clove garlic, finely chopped

Two 6-inch flour tortillas

¼ cup refried beans

¼ cup shredded Cheddar cheese

Vegetable oil

2 tablespoons salsa

Crumble pork sausage into 6 × 4 × 1½-inch dish. Cover with waxed paper and microwave on high (100%) until very little pink remains, 30 to 60 seconds; break up and drain. Stir in tomato, chili powder, lemon juice, salt and garlic. Cover tightly and microwave until hot, 30 to 60 seconds; stir.

Wrap tortillas in damp cloth and microwave on high (100%) until softened, 30 to 45 seconds. Spread 2 tablespoons refried beans over each tortilla. Spoon 2 tablespoons sausage mixture onto center; sprinkle with 2 tablespoons cheese. Roll up. Arrange tortillas, seam sides down, in dish. Brush tops with oil. Cover tightly and microwave until hot, 1½ to 2 minutes. Spoon salsa over tortillas.

2 SERVINGS

4 ounces bulk pork sausage

¼ cup coarsely chopped tomato

2 teaspoons chili powder

2 teaspoons lemon juice

⅛ teaspoon salt

1 small clove garlic, finely chopped

Four 6-inch flour tortillas

½ cup refried beans

½ cup shredded Cheddar cheese

Vegetable oil

¼ cup salsa

Crumble pork sausage into 8 × 8 × 2-inch dish. Cover with waxed paper and microwave on high (100%) until very little pink remains, 1¼ to 1½ minutes; break up and drain. Stir in tomato, chili powder, lemon juice, salt and garlic. Cover tightly and microwave until hot, 1½ to 2 minutes; stir.

Wrap tortillas in damp cloth and microwave on high (100%) until softened, 45 to 60 seconds. Spread 2 tablespoons refried beans over each tortilla. Spoon 2 tablespoons sausage mixture onto center; sprinkle with 2 tablespoons cheese. Roll up. Arrange tortillas, seam sides down, in dish. Brush tops with oil. Cover tightly and microwave until hot, 2½ to 3 minutes. Spoon salsa over tortillas.

Sausage-Vegetable Kabobs

1 SERVING

1 small whole onion, cut into fourths
3 ounces fully cooked kielbasa, cut into 4 pieces
Four ½-inch pieces zucchini
2 medium mushrooms
2 tablespoons taco sauce
1 teaspoon vegetable oil
2 cherry tomatoes

Alternate onion pieces, kielbasa, zucchini pieces and mushrooms on each of 2 wooden skewers, placing onion pieces on ends and mushrooms in centers. Mix taco sauce and oil; brush over kabobs. Place on 10-inch plate. Cover with waxed paper and microwave on high (100%) 1¼ minutes; rearrange kabobs. Cover with waxed paper and microwave until hot, 1¼ to 2¼ minutes longer. Place cherry tomatoes on ends of skewers. Cover with waxed paper and microwave until tomatoes are warm, 30 to 45 seconds. Serve with rice if desired.

2 SERVINGS

2 small whole onions, cut into fourths
6 ounces fully cooked kielbasa, cut into 8 pieces
Eight ½-inch pieces zucchini
4 medium mushrooms
¼ cup taco sauce
2 teaspoons vegetable oil
4 cherry tomatoes

Alternate onion pieces, kielbasa, zucchini pieces and mushrooms on each of 4 wooden skewers, placing onion pieces on ends and mushrooms in centers. Mix taco sauce and oil; brush over kabobs. Place on 10-inch plate. Cover with waxed paper and microwave on high (100%) 2 minutes; rearrange kabobs. Cover with waxed paper and microwave until hot, 2 to 3 minutes longer. Place cherry tomatoes on ends of skewers. Cover with waxed paper and microwave until tomatoes are warm, 45 to 60 seconds. Serve with rice if desired.

Saucy Veal Cutlet

1 SERVING

3-ounce veal cutlet (½ inch thick)
½ cup spaghetti sauce
1 can (2 ounces) mushroom stems and pieces, drained
Snipped parsley

Flatten veal cutlet to ¼-inch thickness between waxed papers; cut into halves. Place veal in 22-ounce casserole; top with spaghetti sauce.

2 SERVINGS

Two 3-ounce veal cutlets (½ inch thick)
1 cup spaghetti sauce
1 can (4 ounces) mushroom stems and pieces, drained
Snipped parsley

Flatten veal cutlets to ¼-inch thickness between waxed papers; cut into halves. Place veal in 8 × 8 × 2-inch dish; top with spaghetti sauce. Cover

Cover with waxed paper and microwave on medium (50%) 2½ minutes; rearrange veal. Cover with waxed paper and microwave until veal is tender, 2½ to 5 minutes longer. Top with mushrooms. Cover with waxed paper and microwave until hot, 30 to 60 seconds. Sprinkle with parsley. Sprinkle with grated Parmesan cheese and serve on hot cooked linguine if desired.

with waxed paper and microwave on medium (50%) 4½ minutes; rearrange veal. Cover with waxed paper and microwave until veal is tender, 4½ to 6½ minutes longer. Top with mushrooms. Cover with waxed paper and microwave until hot, 1½ to 2 minutes. Sprinkle with parsley. Sprinkle with grated Parmesan cheese and serve on hot cooked linguine if desired.

Lamb Loaf with Kiwifruit-Mint Sauce

1 SERVING

Kiwifruit-Mint Sauce (below)
¼ pound ground lamb
3 tablespoons soft bread crumbs
2 tablespoons dry red wine
⅛ teaspoon salt
Dash of dried rosemary, crushed
½ small clove garlic, finely chopped

Prepare Kiwifruit-Mint Sauce. Mix remaining ingredients. Shape into 4 × 2-inch loaf in greased shallow 10-ounce casserole. Microwave uncovered on high (100%) 2 minutes; rotate casserole ¼ turn. Microwave uncovered until almost done, 1 to 2 minutes longer. Let stand uncovered 3 minutes. Serve with Kiwifruit-Mint Sauce. Garnish with mint leaves if desired.

2 SERVINGS

Kiwifruit-Mint Sauce (below)
½ pound ground lamb
⅓ cup soft bread crumbs
¼ cup dry red wine
¼ teaspoon salt
⅛ teaspoon dried rosemary, crushed
1 small clove garlic, finely chopped

Prepare Kiwifruit-Mint Sauce. Mix remaining ingredients. Shape into 6 × 3-inch loaf in greased 9 × 1¼-inch pie plate. Microwave uncovered on high (100%) 2 minutes; rotate pie plate ¼ turn. Microwave uncovered until almost done, 2 to 3 minutes longer. Let stand uncovered 3 minutes. Serve with Kiwifruit-Mint Sauce. Garnish with mint leaves if desired.

KIWIFRUIT-MINT SAUCE

¼ kiwifruit, pared and mashed (1 tablespoon)
1 teaspoon snipped fresh or ⅛ teaspoon dried mint, crushed
½ teaspoon sugar
½ teaspoon lime juice

Mix all ingredients.

½ kiwifruit, pared and mashed (2 tablespoons)
2 teaspoons snipped fresh or ¼ teaspoon dried mint, crushed
1 teaspoon sugar
1 teaspoon lime juice

Mix all ingredients.

Chicken-Pasta Primavera

1 SERVING

1 boneless, skinless chicken breast half
  (about 3 ounces)
½ cup broccoli flowerets
¼ cup ¼-inch-thick strips carrot
½ clove garlic, finely chopped
¾ cup hot cooked fettuccine
1 tablespoon grated Parmesan cheese
1 tablespoon creamy ranch-style dressing
1 tablespoon half-and-half or milk
Dash of dried basil

Cut chicken breast half crosswise into 1-inch strips. Place chicken, broccoli, carrot and garlic in 24-ounce casserole. Cover tightly and microwave on high (100%) 1½ minutes; stir. Cover tightly and microwave until vegetables are tender and chicken is done, 1 to 1½ minutes longer. Toss chicken, vegetables and remaining ingredients. Microwave uncovered until hot, 30 to 40 seconds.

2 SERVINGS

2 boneless, skinless chicken breast halves
  (about 3 ounces each)
1 cup broccoli flowerets
½ cup ¼-inch-thick strips carrot
1 clove garlic, finely chopped
1½ cups hot cooked fettuccine
2 tablespoons grated Parmesan cheese
2 tablespoons creamy ranch-style dressing
2 tablespoons half-and-half or milk
⅛ teaspoon dried basil

Cut chicken breast halves crosswise into 1-inch strips. Place chicken, broccoli, carrot and garlic in 1-quart casserole. Cover tightly and microwave on high (100%) 3 minutes; stir. Cover tightly and microwave until vegetables are tender and chicken is done, 2 to 3 minutes longer. Toss chicken, vegetables and remaining ingredients. Microwave uncovered until hot, 1 to 1½ minutes.

Poached Chicken Breast

Place 8-ounce chicken breast half, skin side up, in 1-quart casserole. Cover tightly and microwave on high (100%) until thickest part is done, 3½ to 4 minutes. Refrigerate until cool enough to handle, about 10 minutes.

Slice and serve, or skin chicken, remove meat from bones and cut up for use in recipes that call for cooked chicken. About ½ cup cut-up chicken.

Chicken-Pasta Primavera

Hot Chicken Salad

1 SERVING

- 1 boneless, skinless chicken breast half (about 3 ounces)
- 2 tablespoons teriyaki sauce
- 1 cup bite-size pieces salad greens
- ¼ cup sliced water chestnuts
- 1 green onion (with top), cut into ½-inch pieces
- ½ can (8-ounce size) pineapple chunks, drained
- 1 tablespoon vegetable oil
- 1 teaspoon teriyaki sauce

Place chicken breast half in shallow glass or plastic dish; pour 2 tablespoons teriyaki sauce over chicken. Cover and refrigerate, turning occasionally, at least 30 minutes but no longer than 24 hours.

Mix salad greens, water chestnuts, onion and pineapple. Mix vegetable oil and 1 teaspoon teriyaki sauce; pour over salad greens and toss. Arrange on salad plate. Place chicken on another plate; cover tightly and microwave on high (100%) until thickest part is done, 2 to 3 minutes. Slice chicken; place on salad greens.

2 SERVINGS

- 2 boneless, skinless chicken breast halves (about 3 ounces each)
- ¼ cup teriyaki sauce
- 2 cups bite-size pieces salad greens
- ½ cup sliced water chestnuts
- 2 green onions (with tops), cut into ½-inch pieces
- 1 can (8 ounces) pineapple chunks, drained
- 2 tablespoons vegetable oil
- 2 teaspoons teriyaki sauce

Place chicken breast halves in shallow glass or plastic dish; pour ¼ cup teriyaki sauce over chicken. Cover and refrigerate, turning occasionally, at least 30 minutes but no longer than 24 hours.

Mix salad greens, water chestnuts, onion and pineapple. Mix vegetable oil and 2 teaspoons teriyaki sauce; pour over salad greens and toss. Arrange on 2 salad plates. Place chicken on another plate with thickest parts to outside edge; cover tightly and microwave on high (100%) until thickest parts are done, 3 to 4 minutes. Slice chicken; place on salad greens.

Hot Chicken Salad

Haddock Caribbean

1 SERVING

1 piece (3 ounces) fresh or frozen (thawed) haddock fillet
Dash of salt
Dash of pepper
1/8-inch-thick slice medium onion, separated into rings
1/2 small tomato, cut into 4 wedges
1 teaspoon lime juice
1 teaspoon olive oil or vegetable oil
2 pitted green olives, sliced
2 slices avocado
1 lime wedge

Place haddock in 12-ounce shallow casserole. Sprinkle with salt and pepper. Place onion and tomato on haddock; sprinkle with lime juice and oil. Top with olives. Cover loosely and microwave on high (100%) until haddock flakes easily with fork, 2 to 3 minutes. Serve with avocado and lime.

2 SERVINGS

2 pieces (3 ounces each) fresh or frozen (thawed) haddock fillet
1/8 teaspoon salt
Dash of pepper
Two 1/8-inch-thick slices medium onion, separated into rings
1 small tomato, cut into 8 wedges
2 teaspoons lime juice
2 teaspoons olive oil or vegetable oil
4 pitted green olives, sliced
4 slices avocado
2 lime wedges

Place haddock in 24-ounce shallow casserole with thickest parts toward outside edges. Sprinkle with salt and pepper. Place onion and tomato on haddock; sprinkle with lime juice and oil. Top with olives. Cover loosely and microwave on high (100%) until haddock flakes easily with fork, 4 to 5 minutes. Serve with avocado and lime.

Haddock Caribbean and Potato with Toppers (page 105)

Wine-poached Salmon Steak

1 SERVING

Prepare Wine-poached Salmon Steak for 2 Servings. Serve any remaining salmon at another meal.

2 SERVINGS

1 fresh or frozen (thawed) salmon steak (6 ounces)
2 tablespoons dry white wine
2 tablespoons water
⅛ teaspoon salt
⅛ teaspoon pepper
⅛ teaspoon dried thyme
⅛ teaspoon dried tarragon
2 lemon slices (⅛ inch thick)

Place salmon steak in 14-ounce shallow casserole. Sprinkle with wine, water, salt, pepper, thyme and tarragon. Top with lemon slices. Cover with waxed paper and microwave on high (100%) until salmon flakes easily with fork, 3 to 5 minutes. Remove from casserole before serving.

Sole on Deviled Stuffing

1 SERVING

1 piece (3 ounces) fresh or frozen (thawed) sole fillet
1½ teaspoons margarine or butter, melted
1 teaspoon lemon juice
⅛ teaspoon dry mustard
⅛ teaspoon chili powder
⅛ teaspoon salt
⅛ teaspoon instant minced onion
¼ cup soft bread crumbs
1 teaspoon margarine or butter, melted
⅛ teaspoon paprika

2 SERVINGS

2 pieces (3 ounces each) fresh or frozen (thawed) sole fillet
1 tablespoon margarine or butter, melted
2 teaspoons lemon juice
¼ teaspoon dry mustard
¼ teaspoon chili powder
¼ teaspoon salt
¼ teaspoon instant minced onion
½ cup soft bread crumbs
2 teaspoons margarine or butter, melted
¼ teaspoon paprika

Pat sole dry. Mix 1½ teaspoons margarine, the lemon juice, mustard, chili powder, salt and onion; stir in bread crumbs. Spread in 12-ounce shallow casserole. Place sole on top. Mix 1 teaspoon margarine and the paprika; spread over sole. Cover with waxed paper and microwave on high (100%) until sole flakes easily with fork, 1 to 2 minutes.

Pat sole pieces dry. Mix 1 tablespoon margarine, the lemon juice, mustard, chili powder, salt and onion; stir in bread crumbs. Spread in two 12-ounce shallow casseroles. Place sole on top. Mix 2 teaspoons margarine and the paprika; spread over sole. Cover with waxed paper and microwave on high (100%) until sole flakes easily with fork, 2 to 3 minutes.

Shrimp-Vegetable Oriental

1 SERVING

¾ cup frozen broccoli, carrots and cauliflower
1½ teaspoons vegetable oil
½ clove garlic, finely chopped
½ green onion, sliced
3 drops red pepper sauce
2 ounces frozen cooked shrimp, thawed
⅛ teaspoon cornstarch
½ teaspoon soy sauce
⅛ teaspoon sesame seed
Dash of ground ginger

Place frozen vegetables, oil, garlic, onion and pepper sauce in 24-ounce casserole. Cover and microwave on high (100%) until vegetables are crisp-tender, 2 to 2½ minutes. Stir in remaining ingredients. Cover and microwave 30 seconds; stir. Cover and microwave on medium (50%) until hot, 45 to 60 seconds longer. Serve with hot cooked rice if desired.

2 SERVINGS

1½ cups frozen broccoli, carrots and cauliflower
1 tablespoon vegetable oil
1 clove garlic, finely chopped
1 green onion, sliced
6 drops red pepper sauce
4 ounces frozen cooked shrimp, thawed
¼ teaspoon cornstarch
1 teaspoon soy sauce
¼ teaspoon sesame seed
Dash of ground ginger

Place frozen vegetables, oil, garlic, onion and pepper sauce in 1-quart casserole. Cover and microwave on high (100%) until vegetables are crisp-tender, 4 to 5 minutes. Stir in remaining ingredients. Cover and microwave 1 minute; stir. Cover and microwave on medium (50%) until hot, 1 to 1½ minutes longer. Serve with hot cooked rice if desired.

Spaghetti with Tuna Sauce

1 SERVING

1½ teaspoons margarine or butter
½ small clove garlic, finely chopped
¼ cup half-and-half
1 tablespoon grated Parmesan cheese
⅛ teaspoon dried oregano
⅛ teaspoon salt
⅛ teaspoon white pepper
½ can (6½-ounce size) tuna, drained
4 pitted ripe olives, sliced
¾ cup hot cooked thin spaghetti

Place margarine and garlic in 2-cup measure. Microwave uncovered on high (100%) until margarine is melted, about 30 seconds. Stir in remaining ingredients except spaghetti. Cover with waxed paper and microwave until bubbly, 1½ to 2 minutes. Toss with hot spaghetti. Sprinkle with snipped parsley if desired.

2 SERVINGS

1 tablespoon margarine or butter
1 small clove garlic, finely chopped
½ cup half-and-half
2 tablespoons grated Parmesan cheese
¼ teaspoon dried oregano
¼ teaspoon salt
¼ teaspoon white pepper
1 can (6½ ounces) tuna, drained
8 pitted ripe olives, sliced
1½ cups hot cooked thin spaghetti

Place margarine and garlic in 4-cup measure. Microwave uncovered on high (100%) until margarine is melted, about 45 seconds. Stir in remaining ingredients except spaghetti. Cover with waxed paper and microwave until bubbly, 2½ to 3 minutes. Toss with hot spaghetti. Sprinkle with snipped parsley if desired.

Gingered Scallops

1 SERVING

1 tablespoon chopped green onion (with top)
1½ teaspoons margarine or butter
1½ teaspoons all-purpose flour
¼ cup half-and-half
1 tablespoon dry white wine
¼ teaspoon grated gingerroot
⅛ teaspoon salt
3 ounces bay scallops or sea scallops, cut into ½-inch pieces (⅓ cup)
1 jar (2½ ounces) whole mushrooms, drained

Place onion and margarine in 2-cup measure.

2 SERVINGS

2 tablespoons chopped green onion (with top)
1 tablespoon margarine or butter
1 tablespoon all-purpose flour
½ cup half-and-half
2 tablespoons dry white wine
½ teaspoon grated gingerroot
¼ teaspoon salt
6 ounces bay scallops or sea scallops, cut into ½-inch pieces (⅔ cup)
1 jar (4½ ounces) whole mushrooms, drained

Place onion and margarine in 4-cup measure.

Microwave uncovered on high (100%) until margarine is melted, about 30 seconds. Mix in flour. Stir in half-and-half, wine, gingerroot and salt. Microwave uncovered 30 seconds; stir. Microwave until thickened, about 30 seconds longer. Stir in scallops and mushrooms. Spoon into 14-ounce shallow casserole. Cover tightly and microwave on medium-high (70%), rotating casserole ½ turn every minute, until bubbly, 2 to 3 minutes. Sprinkle with grated lime peel and serve with hot cooked rice if desired.

Microwave uncovered on high (100%) until margarine is melted, about 1 minute. Mix in flour. Stir in half-and-half, wine, gingerroot and salt. Microwave uncovered 1 minute; stir. Microwave until thickened, about 1 minute longer. Stir in scallops and mushrooms. Spoon into two 14-ounce shallow casseroles. Cover tightly and microwave on medium-high (70%), rotating casseroles ½ turn every minute, until bubbly, 4 to 5 minutes. Sprinkle with grated lime peel and serve with hot cooked rice if desired.

Salmon Tetrazzini

1 SERVING

1 teaspoon dry white wine
Milk
½ can (7¾-ounce size) salmon, drained (reserve 2 tablespoons liquid)
1½ teaspoons margarine or butter
1½ teaspoons all-purpose flour
⅛ teaspoon salt
¾ cup hot cooked spaghetti
1 tablespoon grated Parmesan cheese
Dash of ground nutmeg
2 mushrooms, sliced
1 tablespoon sliced almonds, toasted (page 7)

Add wine and enough milk to reserved salmon liquid to measure ½ cup; reserve. Microwave margarine uncovered in 24-ounce casserole on high (100%) until melted, about 30 seconds. Mix in flour. Stir in salt and reserved wine mixture. Microwave uncovered, stirring every 30 seconds, until thickened, 2½ to 3 minutes. Stir in salmon, spaghetti, cheese, nutmeg and mushrooms. Sprinkle with almonds. Microwave uncovered until hot, 2 to 2½ minutes.

2 SERVINGS

2 teaspoons dry white wine
Milk
1 can (7¾ ounces) salmon, drained (reserve ¼ cup liquid)
1 tablespoon margarine or butter
1 tablespoon all-purpose flour
¼ teaspoon salt
1½ cups hot cooked spaghetti
2 tablespoons grated Parmesan cheese
⅛ teaspoon ground nutmeg
4 mushrooms, sliced
2 tablespoons sliced almonds, toasted (page 7)

Add wine and enough milk to reserved salmon liquid to measure 1 cup; reserve. Microwave margarine uncovered in 1-quart casserole on high (100%) until melted, about 45 seconds. Mix in flour. Stir in salt and reserved wine mixture. Microwave uncovered, stirring every 30 seconds, until thickened, 3 to 4 minutes. Stir in salmon, spaghetti, cheese, nutmeg and mushrooms. Sprinkle with almonds. Microwave uncovered until hot, 5 to 6 minutes.

Ham Quiche

1 SERVING

Cornmeal Quiche Shell (page 94)
3 tablespoons shredded mozzarella cheese
1½ teaspoons finely chopped green onion (with top)
1 egg
3 tablespoons milk
⅛ teaspoon salt
3 drops red pepper sauce
1 tablespoon finely chopped fully cooked smoked ham

Microwave Cornmeal Quiche Shell. Sprinkle cheese and onion in shell. Beat egg, milk, salt and pepper sauce with fork in 2-cup measure; stir in ham. Microwave uncovered on medium-high (70%) until warm, 1 to 1½ minutes. Stir; pour into shell. Place shell on inverted saucer in microwave oven. Microwave uncovered on medium-high (70%) 2 minutes; rotate dish ½ turn. Microwave uncovered until center is almost set, 1 to 2 minutes longer. Cover loosely and let stand on flat, heatproof surface 3 minutes.

2 SERVINGS

Cornmeal Quiche Shells (page 94)
⅓ cup shredded mozzarella cheese
1 tablespoon finely chopped green onion (with top)
2 eggs
⅓ cup milk
¼ teaspoon salt
6 drops red pepper sauce
2 tablespoons finely chopped fully cooked smoked ham

Microwave Cornmeal Quiche Shells. Sprinkle cheese and onion in shells. Beat eggs, milk, salt and pepper sauce with fork in 2-cup measure; stir in ham. Microwave uncovered on medium-high (70%) 1 minute; stir. Microwave uncovered until warm, 2 to 3 minutes longer. Stir; pour into shells. Place shells on inverted saucers in microwave oven. Microwave uncovered on medium-high (70%) 2 minutes; rotate dishes ½ turn. Microwave uncovered until center is almost set, 2 to 3 minutes longer. Cover loosely and let stand on flat, heatproof surface 3 minutes.

Ham Quiche

Savory Broccoli

1 SERVING

2 spears broccoli (1 ounce)
2 teaspoons water
1½ teaspoons margarine or butter
¼ teaspoon prepared horseradish
Dash of salt
Dash of dry mustard

Cut broccoli lengthwise into thin pieces. Arrange broccoli in 22-ounce casserole with tips in center; add water. Cover tightly and microwave on high (100%) 1 minute; rotate casserole ½ turn. Microwave until tender, 1½ to 2 minutes longer. Let stand covered 1 minute; drain.

Place remaining ingredients in 6-ounce custard cup. Cover with vented plastic wrap and microwave on high (100%) until margarine is melted, about 15 seconds; stir. Pour over broccoli. Sprinkle with paprika if desired.

2 SERVINGS

4 spears broccoli (2 ounces)
1 tablespoon water
1 tablespoon margarine or butter
½ teaspoon prepared horseradish
⅛ teaspoon salt
⅛ teaspoon dry mustard

Cut broccoli lengthwise into thin pieces. Arrange broccoli in 9 × 1¼-inch pie plate with tips in center; add water. Cover tightly and microwave on high (100%) 1 minute; rotate pie plate ½ turn. Microwave until tender, 4 to 4½ minutes longer. Let stand covered 1 minute; drain.

Place remaining ingredients in 6-ounce custard cup. Cover with vented plastic wrap and microwave on high (100%) until margarine is melted, about 30 seconds; stir. Pour over broccoli. Sprinkle with paprika if desired.

Creamy Cabbage

1 SERVING

1 tablespoon water
¼ teaspoon celery salt
Dash of garlic powder
1½ cups finely shredded green cabbage
2 tablespoons whipped cream cheese
2 teaspoons milk
⅛ teaspoon celery seed
Freshly ground pepper

Mix water, celery salt, garlic powder and cabbage in 16-ounce casserole. Cover with vented plastic wrap and microwave on high (100%) until crisp-tender, 2 to 3 minutes. Mix remaining ingredients; stir into hot cabbage.

2 SERVINGS

2 tablespoons water
½ teaspoon celery salt
Dash of garlic powder
3 cups finely shredded green cabbage
¼ cup whipped cream cheese
1 tablespoon plus 1 teaspoon milk
¼ teaspoon celery seed
Freshly ground pepper

Mix water, celery salt, garlic powder and cabbage in 1-quart casserole. Cover with vented plastic wrap and microwave on high (100%) until crisp-tender, 3 to 4 minutes. Mix remaining ingredients; stir into hot cabbage.

Shredded Carrots

1 SERVING

1 slice bacon, cut into ½-inch pieces
¾ cup coarsely shredded carrot (1 large)
1 finely chopped green onion (with top)
1 teaspoon lemon juice
Dash of salt
Dash of pepper

Place bacon in 2-cup measure. Cover loosely and microwave on high (100%) until crisp, 2 to 2½ minutes. Remove bacon with slotted spoon; crumble and reserve.

Stir remaining ingredients into bacon fat. Cover with vented plastic wrap and microwave until crip-tender, 2½ to 3 minutes. Sprinkle with reserved bacon.

2 SERVINGS

2 slices bacon, cut into ½-inch pieces
1½ cups coarsely shredded carrots (2 large)
2 finely chopped green onions (with tops)
2 teaspoons lemon juice
Dash of salt
Dash of pepper

Place bacon in 4-cup measure. Cover loosely and microwave on high (100%) until crisp, 3 to 3½ minutes. Remove bacon with slotted spoon; crumble and reserve.

Stir remaining ingredients into bacon fat. Cover with vented plastic wrap and microwave until crisp-tender, 3½ to 4 minutes. Sprinkle with reserved bacon.

Glazed Carrots

1 SERVING

¾ cup ¼-inch slices carrots
1 tablespoon packed brown sugar
½ teaspoon cornstarch
Dash of ground cinnamon
3 tablespoons orange juice
1½ teaspoons margarine or butter

Place carrots in 12-ounce casserole. Mix brown sugar, cornstarch and cinnamon; stir in orange juice. Pour over carrots; dot with margarine. Cover with vented plastic wrap and microwave on high (100%) 3 minutes; stir. Cover with vented plastic wrap and microwave until crisp-tender, 1 to 3 minutes longer.

2 SERVINGS

1½ cups ¼-inch slices carrots
2 tablespoons packed brown sugar
1 teaspoon cornstarch
⅛ teaspoon ground cinnamon
⅓ cup orange juice
1 tablespoon margarine or butter

Place carrots in 24-ounce casserole. Mix brown sugar, cornstarch and cinnamon; stir in orange juice. Pour over carrots; dot with margarine. Cover with vented plastic wrap and microwave on high (100%) 4 minutes; stir. Cover with vented plastic wrap and microwave until crisp-tender, 2 to 4 minutes longer.

Zippy Cauliflower

1 SERVING

3 large cauliflowerets (about 1¾ inches each)
2 teaspoons sour cream
1½ teaspoons process jalapeño pepper cheese spread
Dash of seasoned salt

Place cauliflower on 4-inch plate. Cover with vented plastic wrap and microwave on high (100%) until crisp-tender, 1½ to 2 minutes; drain. Spread sour cream over cauliflower. Spoon cheese onto sour cream; sprinkle with seasoned salt. Microwave uncovered until cheese is melted, 15 to 20 seconds.

2 SERVINGS

6 large cauliflowerets (about 1¾ inches each)
1 tablespoon sour cream
1 tablespoon process jalapeño pepper cheese spread
Dash of seasoned salt

Place cauliflower on 6-inch plate. Cover with vented plastic wrap and microwave on high (100%) until crisp-tender, 3 to 3½ minutes; drain. Spread sour cream over cauliflower. Spoon cheese onto sour cream; sprinkle with seasoned salt. Microwave uncovered until cheese is melted, 30 to 40 seconds.

Peppery Corn and Tomatoes

1 SERVING

1 teaspoon water
⅛ teaspoon garlic powder
⅛ teaspoon salt
Dash of ground red pepper
⅔ cup frozen whole kernel corn
1 green onion (with top), chopped
1 teaspoon margarine or butter
¼ medium tomato, chopped

Place water, garlic powder, salt, red pepper, corn and onion in 12-ounce casserole. Cover with vented plastic wrap and microwave on high (100%) until corn is tender 2½ to 3½ minutes. Stir in margarine and tomato. Cover with vented plastic wrap and microwave until tomato is hot, about 30 seconds.

2 SERVINGS

2 teaspoons water
¼ teaspoon garlic powder
¼ teaspoon salt
Dash of ground red pepper
1⅓ cups frozen whole kernel corn
2 green onions (with tops), chopped
2 teaspoons margarine or butter
½ medium tomato, chopped

Place water, garlic powder, salt, red pepper, corn and onion in 24-ounce casserole. Cover with vented plastic wrap and microwave on high (100%) until corn is tender, 4 to 5 minutes. Stir in margarine and tomato. Cover with vented plastic wrap and microwave until tomato is hot, about 1 minute.

Peppery Corn and Tomatoes

Mushrooms in Wine

1 SERVING

1 teaspoon margarine or butter
½ teaspoon cornstarch
Dash of salt
1 tablespoon dry white wine
4 ounces mushrooms, cut into halves
   (1½ cups)
½ small clove garlic, finely chopped
Snipped parsley

Place all ingredients except parsley in 16-ounce casserole. Cover loosely and microwave on high (100%) 1 minute; stir. Cover loosely and microwave until hot, 30 to 60 seconds longer. Sprinkle with parsley.

2 SERVINGS

2 teaspoons margarine or butter
1 teaspoon cornstarch
⅛ teaspoon salt
2 tablespoons dry white wine
8 ounces mushrooms, cut into halves
   (3 cups)
1 small clove garlic, finely chopped
Snipped parsley

Place all ingredients except parsley in 1-quart casserole. Cover loosely and microwave on high (100%) 2 minutes; stir. Cover loosely and microwave until hot, 1 to 1½ minutes longer. Sprinkle with parsley.

Stuffed Potato

1 SERVING

1 large baking potato
2 tablespoons milk
2 tablespoons sour cream
1 tablespoon margarine or butter
2 tablespoons shredded dried beef
1 tablespoon finely chopped green onion
   (with top)
Dash of salt
Dash of pepper
2 tablespoons shredded process American
   cheese

Prick potato with fork to allow steam to escape. Microwave uncovered on high (100%) 3 minutes; turn potato over. Microwave uncovered until tender, 2 to 4 minutes longer. Wrap potato in aluminum foil; let stand 5 minutes.

2 SERVINGS

2 large baking potatoes
¼ cup milk
¼ cup sour cream
2 tablespoons margarine or butter
¼ cup shredded dried beef
2 tablespoons finely chopped green onion
   (with top)
⅛ teaspoon salt
⅛ teaspoon pepper
¼ cup shredded process American cheese

Prick potatoes with fork to allow steam to escape. Microwave uncovered on high (100%) 3 minutes; turn potatoes over. Microwave uncovered until tender, 4 to 6 minutes longer. Wrap potatoes in aluminum foil; let stand 5 minutes.

Cut thin lengthwise slice from top of potato; scoop out inside, leaving thin shell. Mash potato, milk, sour cream and margarine. Stir in beef, onion, salt and pepper. Fill shell with potato mixture; place on plate. Cover with waxed paper and microwave on medium (50%) until hot, 2 to 3 minutes. Sprinkle with cheese. Microwave uncovered on high (100%) until cheese is melted, about 30 seconds.

Cut thin lengthwise slice from tops of potatoes; scoop out insides, leaving thin shells. Mash potato, milk, sour cream and margarine. Stir in beef, onion, salt and pepper. Fill shells with potato mixture; place on plate. Cover with waxed paper and microwave on medium (50%) until hot, 4 to 5 minutes. Sprinkle with cheese. Microwave uncovered on high (100%) until cheese is melted, about 1 minute.

Potato with Toppers

1 SERVING

1 medium baking potato
Toppers (below)

Prick potato with fork to allow steam to escape. Microwave uncovered on high (100%) 3 minutes; turn potato over. Microwave uncovered until tender, 1½ to 2 minutes longer. Wrap potato in aluminum foil; let stand 5 minutes. Slit top of potato and squeeze open; top with one of the Toppers.

2 SERVINGS

2 medium baking potatoes
Toppers (below)

Prick potatoes with fork to allow steam to escape. Microwave uncovered on high (100%) 3 minutes; turn potatoes over. Microwave uncovered until tender, 3½ to 5 minutes longer. Wrap potatoes in aluminum foil; let stand 5 minutes. Slit tops of potatoes and squeeze open; top with one of the Toppers.

TOPPERS

Dairy sour cream and finely chopped green onion (with top)

Hot cooked chopped broccoli and shredded mozzarella cheese

Hot chili and shredded Cheddar cheese

Diced fully cooked smoked ham and chili sauce

Crisply cooked bacon pieces and shredded American cheese

Flaked canned tuna and sour cream or mayonnaise

Chopped canned shrimp, whipped cream cheese and chives

Easy Scalloped Potatoes

1 SERVING

1 medium potato, pared and sliced ⅛ inch thick
Two ⅛-inch-thick slices medium onion, separated into rings
⅛ teaspoon salt
2 teaspoons water
2 teaspoons margarine or butter
2 tablespoons milk or half-and-half
2 teaspoons grated Parmesan cheese
Dash of paprika

Layer potato and onion slices alternately in 10-ounce casserole; sprinkle with salt. Spoon water over potato slices; dot with margarine. Cover and microwave on high (100%) until almost tender, 4 to 5 minutes; stir in milk. Sprinkle with cheese and paprika. Microwave uncovered until bubbly, 45 to 60 seconds.

2 SERVINGS

2 medium potatoes, pared and sliced ⅛ inch thick
Four ⅛-inch-thick slices medium onion, separated into rings
¼ teaspoon salt
1 tablespoon water
1 tablespoon margarine or butter
3 tablespoons milk or half-and-half
1 tablespoon grated Parmesan cheese
Dash of paprika

Layer potato and onion slices alternately in 20-ounce casserole; sprinkle with salt. Spoon water over potato slices; dot with margarine. Cover and microwave on high (100%) until almost tender, 7 to 8 minutes; stir in milk. Sprinkle with cheese and paprika. Microwave uncovered until bubbly, 1½ to 2 minutes.

Sweet Potato with Maple-Nut Topping

1 SERVING

1 medium sweet potato
1 tablespoon margarine or butter
1 tablespoon maple-flavored syrup
1 tablespoon chopped pecans

Prick potato with fork to allow steam to escape. Microwave uncovered on high (100%) 3 minutes; turn potato over. Microwave uncovered until tender, 1½ to 2 minutes longer. Wrap in aluminum foil; let stand 5 minutes.

Slit top of potato and squeeze open; top with margarine. Drizzle with syrup; sprinkle with chopped pecans.

2 SERVINGS

2 medium sweet potatoes
2 tablespoons margarine or butter
2 tablespoons maple-flavored syrup
2 tablespoons chopped pecans

Prick potatoes with fork to allow steam to escape. Microwave uncovered on high (100%) 3 minutes; turn potatoes over. Microwave uncovered until tender, 2½ to 4 minutes longer. Wrap in aluminum foil; let stand 5 minutes.

Slit tops of potatoes and squeeze open; top with margarine. Drizzle with syrup; sprinkle with chopped pecans.

Pasta

1 SERVING

2 ounces uncooked small pasta*
  (about ½ cup)
¼ teaspoon salt
2 cups hot water

Mix pasta, salt and water in 1-quart casserole. Microwave uncovered on high (100%) until boiling, 3½ to 5 minutes; stir. Microwave uncovered on medium (50%) until tender, 6 to 8 minutes longer; drain.

2 SERVINGS

4 ounces uncooked small pasta*
  (about 1 cup)
½ teaspoon salt
3 cups hot water

Mix pasta, salt and water in 1½-quart casserole. Microwave uncovered on high (100%) until boiling, 6½ to 8 minutes; stir. Microwave uncovered on medium (50%) until tender, 6 to 8 minutes longer; drain.

*Elbow macaroni, small macaroni shells or medium noodles. If using noodles, increase amount to 1 cup for 1 Serving, 2 cups for 2 Servings.

Vermicelli Parmesan

1 SERVING

1½ ounces vermicelli
1 tablespoon half-and-half or milk
2 teaspoons margarine or butter
Dash of garlic salt
Dash of dried basil
1 tablespoon grated Parmesan cheese

Cook vermicelli as directed on package; drain. Place vermicelli in 16-ounce casserole; mix in remaining ingredients except cheese. Microwave uncovered on high (100%) until hot, 20 to 30 seconds. Mix in cheese.

2 SERVINGS

3 ounces vermicelli
2 tablespoons half-and-half or milk
1 tablespoon margarine or butter
⅛ teaspoon garlic salt
⅛ teaspoon dried basil
2 tablespoons grated Parmesan cheese

Cook vermicelli as directed on package; drain. Place vermicelli in 1-quart casserole; mix in remaining ingredients except cheese. Microwave uncovered on high (100%) until hot, 30 to 40 seconds. Mix in cheese.

Rice Pilaf

1 SERVING

3 tablespoons uncooked long grain rice
½ cup water
¼ teaspoon instant chicken bouillon (dry)
¼ teaspoon parsley flakes
1 tablespoon chopped celery
1 green onion (with top), sliced

Mix all ingredients in 10-ounce casserole. Cover tightly and microwave on medium-low (30%) until rice is almost tender, 15 to 17 minutes. Let stand covered 5 minutes.

2 SERVINGS

⅓ cup uncooked long grain rice
¾ cup water
½ teaspoon instant chicken bouillon (dry)
½ teaspoon parsley flakes
2 tablespoons chopped celery
2 green onion (with tops), sliced

Mix all ingredients in 20-ounce casserole. Cover tightly and microwave on medium (50%) until rice is almost tender, 15 to 17 minutes. Let stand covered 5 minutes.

Layered Zucchini and Tomato

1 SERVING

½ cup ¼-inch-thick slices zucchini
1 tablespoon sliced green onion (with top)
Dash of salt
Dash of dried basil
Dash of pepper
½ medium tomato, cut into ½-inch-thick slices
2 tablespoons sour cream
1 teaspoon grated Parmesan cheese

Mix zucchini, onion, salt, basil and pepper in 16-ounce casserole. Cover with waxed paper and microwave on high (100%) until zucchini is crisp-tender, 30 to 60 seconds; stir. Place tomato slices on zucchini. Mix sour cream and cheese; spread over tomato slices. Cover with waxed paper and microwave on medium-low (30%) until tomato slices are warm, 1 to 2 minutes. Sprinkle with additional grated Parmesan cheese if desired.

2 SERVINGS

1 cup ¼-inch-thick slices zucchini
2 tablespoons sliced green onion (with top)
⅛ teaspoon salt
⅛ teaspoon dried basil
Dash of pepper
1 medium tomato, cut into ½-inch-thick slices
¼ cup sour cream
2 teaspoons grated Parmesan cheese

Mix zucchini, onion, salt, basil and pepper in 1-quart casserole. Cover with waxed paper and microwave on high (100%) until zucchini is crisp-tender, 1 to 1½ minutes; stir. Place tomato slices on zucchini. Mix sour cream and cheese; spread over tomato slices. Cover with waxed paper and microwave on medium-low (30%) until tomato slices are warm, 1½ to 2 minutes. Sprinkle with additional grated Parmesan cheese if desired.

Peppers and Mushrooms

1 SERVING

1½ teaspoons margarine or butter
⅛ teaspoon red pepper sauce
Dash of salt
½ medium green pepper, cut into
    ¼-inch-thick strips
⅛-inch-thick slice medium onion, separated
    into rings
3 mushrooms, thinly sliced

Place margarine in 12-ounce shallow casserole. Microwave uncovered on high (100%) until melted, 15 to 25 seconds. Mix in pepper sauce and salt. Stir in remaining ingredients. Cover with vented plastic wrap and microwave until green pepper is crisp-tender, 2 to 3 minutes. Serve over grilled steak if desired.

2 SERVINGS

1 tablespoon margarine or butter
¼ teaspoon red pepper sauce
⅛ teaspoon salt
1 medium green pepper, cut into
    ¼-inch-thick strips
Two ⅛-inch-thick slices medium onion,
    separated into rings
6 mushrooms, thinly sliced

Place margarine in 24-ounce shallow casserole. Microwave uncovered on high (100%) until melted, 30 to 45 seconds. Mix in pepper sauce and salt. Stir in remaining ingredients. Cover with vented plastic wrap and microwave until green pepper is crisp-tender, 3 to 4 minutes. Serve over grilled steak if desired.

Buttercup Squash with Apples

1 SERVING

¼ small buttercup squash (¼ pound)
¼ cup chopped tart apple
1 teaspoon packed brown sugar
1 teaspoon margarine or butter, softened
¼ teaspoon lemon juice
Dash of ground nutmeg

Remove seeds and fibers from squash. Place squash, cut sides up, in 9 × 1¼-inch pie plate. Mix remaining ingredients; spoon into squash. Cover with waxed paper and microwave on high (100%) 1 minute; rotate pie plate ½ turn. Microwave until tender, 1½ to 2½ minutes longer. Spoon juices over squash.

2 SERVINGS

½ small buttercup squash (½ pound)
½ cup chopped tart apple
2 teaspoons packed brown sugar
2 teaspoons margarine or butter, softened
½ teaspoon lemon juice
Dash of ground nutmeg

Remove seeds and fibers from squash; cut in half. Place squash, cut sides up, in 9 × 1¼-inch pie plate. Mix remaining ingredients; spoon into squash pieces. Cover with waxed paper and microwave on high (100%) 2 minutes; rotate pie plate ½ turn. Microwave until tender, 2 to 3 minutes longer. Spoon juices over squash.

Vegetable Combo

1 SERVING

½ cup broccoli flowerets
½ cup cauliflowerets
1½ teaspoons mayonnaise or salad dressing
1½ teaspoons plain yogurt or sour cream
¹⁄₁₆ teaspoon prepared mustard
½ teaspoon imitation bacon pieces

Arrange broccoli and cauliflower in a circle, alternately, on 6-inch plate. Cover with vented plastic wrap and microwave on high (100%) until crisp-tender, 1½ to 2 minutes; drain. Stir mayonnaise, yogurt and mustard in bowl until blended; spoon over vegetables. Sprinkle with imitation bacon. Microwave uncovered until hot, 15 to 20 seconds.

2 SERVINGS

1 cup broccoli flowerets
1 cup cauliflowerets
1 tablespoon mayonnaise or salad dressing
1 tablespoon plain yogurt or sour cream
⅛ teaspoon prepared mustard
1 teaspoon imitation bacon pieces

Arrange broccoli and cauliflower in a circle, alternately, on 8-inch plate. Cover with vented plastic wrap and microwave on high (100%) until crisp-tender, 3 to 3½ minutes; drain. Stir mayonnaise, yogurt and mustard in bowl until blended; spoon over vegetables. Sprinkle with imitation bacon. Microwave uncovered until hot, 20 to 30 seconds.

Zucchini and Carrots with Basil

1 SERVING

½ cup ¼-inch-thick zucchini
2 tablespoons shredded carrot
1½ teaspoons margarine or butter
½ teaspoon snipped fresh basil
Dash of salt
Freshly ground pepper

Mix all ingredients except pepper in 14-ounce casserole. Cover tightly and microwave on high (100%) 30 to 60 seconds; stir. Cover tightly and microwave until crisp-tender, about 30 seconds longer. Sprinkle with pepper.

2 SERVINGS

1 cup ¼-inch-thick slices zucchini
¼ cup shredded carrot
1 tablespoon margarine or butter
1 teaspoon snipped fresh basil
Dash of salt
Freshly ground pepper

Mix all ingredients except pepper in 16-ounce casserole. Cover tightly and microwave on high (100%) 1 to 1½ minutes; stir. Cover tightly and microwave until crisp-tender, about 30 to 60 seconds longer. Sprinkle with pepper.

Vegetable Combo and Zucchini and Carrots with Basil

Caramel-Pecan Coffee Cake

1 SERVING

Prepare Caramel-Pecan Coffee Cake for 2 Servings. Reheat half of the coffee cake for another meal.

2 SERVINGS

2 tablespoons margarine or butter
¼ cup packed brown sugar
2 tablespoons chopped pecans
2 tablespoons light corn syrup
¼ teaspoon ground cinnamon
1 cup baking mix
¼ cup cold water

Place margarine in 1-quart casserole. Microwave uncovered on high (100%) until melted, 20 to 30 seconds. Stir in brown sugar, pecans, corn syrup and cinnamon; spread evenly in casserole. Microwave uncovered until bubbly, 45 to 60 seconds. Tilt casserole so brown sugar mixture runs to side; place 6-ounce juice glass in center of casserole.

Mix baking mix and water until soft dough forms. Drop dough by 6 spoonfuls onto brown sugar mixture. Place casserole on inverted plate in microwave oven. Microwave uncovered on medium-high (70%) 2 minutes; rotate casserole ½ turn. Microwave uncovered until wooden pick inserted in center comes out clean, 2 to 2½ minutes longer. Remove glass. Immediately invert on heatproof serving plate; let casserole stand 1 minute so caramel can drizzle over coffee cake. Serve warm.

Caramel-Pecan Coffee Cake

Delightful Desserts

Honey-Spice Apple

1 SERVING

1 medium cooking apple
1 tablespoon raisins
1 tablespoon honey
⅛ teaspoon ground cinnamon
1 teaspoon margarine or butter

Core apple and pare 1-inch strip of skin from around middle to prevent splitting. Place apple in 10-ounce custard cup. Pack raisins into apple. Mix honey and cinnamon; pour over raisins into apple. Top with margarine. Cover tightly and microwave on high (100%) until tender when pierced with fork, 2 to 2½ minutes. Serve warm with cream if desired.

2 SERVINGS

2 medium cooking apples
2 tablespoons raisins
2 tablespoons honey
¼ teaspoon ground cinnamon
2 teaspoons margarine or butter

Core apples and pare 1-inch strip of skin from around middle of each to prevent splitting. Place apples in two 10-ounce custard cups. Pack raisins into apples. Mix honey and cinnamon; pour over raisins into apples. Top with margarine. Cover tightly and microwave on high (100%) until tender when pierced with fork, 3 to 4 minutes. Serve warm with cream if desired.

Apple Crisp

1 SERVING

¾ cup sliced tart apples
1 tablespoon all-purpose flour
1 tablespoon quick-cooking oats
1 tablespoon packed brown sugar
1 tablespoon margarine or butter, softened
Dash of ground cinnamon
Dash of ground nutmeg

Spread apple slices in 12-ounce casserole. Mix remaining ingredients until crumbly; sprinkle over apple slices. Microwave uncovered on high (100%) until tender, 3 to 3½ minutes. Serve warm with vanilla or cinnamon ice cream if desired.

2 SERVINGS

1½ cups sliced tart apples
2 tablespoons all-purpose flour
2 tablespoons quick-cooking oats
2 tablespoons packed brown sugar
2 tablespoons margarine or butter, softened
⅛ teaspoon ground cinnamon
⅛ teaspooon ground nutmeg

Spread apple slices in 24-ounce casserole. Mix remaining ingredients until crumbly; sprinkle over apple slices. Microwave uncovered on high (100%) until apples are tender, 5 to 6 minutes. Serve warm with vanilla or cinnamon ice cream if desired.

Apple Crisp

Applesauce

1 SERVING

1 medium cooking apple, pared and sliced
2 teaspoons water
2 teaspoons sugar or honey
Dash of ground cinnamon

Place apple and water in 2-cup bowl. Cover with vented plastic wrap and microwave on high (100%) until apple is tender, 2 to 2½ minutes. Stir in sugar and cinnamon until blended. Serve warm or cold.

2 SERVINGS

2 medium cooking apples, pared and sliced
1 tablespoon water
1 tablespoon sugar or honey
⅛ teaspoon ground cinnamon

Place apples and water in 1-quart bowl. Cover with vented plastic wrap and microwave on high (100%) until apples are tender, 3½ to 4 minutes. Stir in sugar and cinnamon until blended. Serve warm or cold.

Flaming Pecan Bananas

1 SERVING

1½ teaspoons margarine or butter
1½ teaspoons honey
Dash of ground nutmeg
½ firm banana, cut lengthwise into halves
1½ teaspoons chopped pecans
1½ teaspoons dark rum

Place margarine in 12-ounce casserole. Microwave uncovered on high (100%) until melted, 10 to 20 seconds. Stir in honey and nutmeg. Place banana in honey mixture; roll to coat. Sprinkle with pecans. Microwave uncovered until hot, 30 to 60 seconds.

Place rum in 1-cup measure. Microwave uncovered on high (100%) until warm, about 10 seconds. Pour rum into metal serving spoon; ignite in spoon and pour over bananas.

2 SERVINGS

1 tablespoon margarine or butter
1 tablespoon honey
⅛ teaspoon ground nutmeg
1 firm banana, cut lengthwise into halves
1 tablespoon chopped pecans
1 tablespoon dark rum

Place margarine in 12-ounce casserole. Microwave uncovered on high (100%) until melted, 25 to 30 seconds. Stir in honey and nutmeg. Place banana in honey mixture; roll to coat. Sprinkle with pecans. Microwave uncovered until hot, 1 to 2 minutes.

Place rum in 1-cup measure. Microwave uncovered on high (100%) until warm, about 15 seconds. Pour rum into metal serving spoon; ignite in spoon and pour over bananas.

Flaming Pecan Bananas

Blueberry Cobbler

1 SERVING

1 tablespoon sugar
½ teaspoon cornstarch
⅔ cup fresh or frozen (thawed) blueberries
1 teaspoon lemon juice
¼ cup baking mix
1 teaspoon sugar
1 tablespoon milk
1 tablespoon dairy sour cream
½ teaspoon sugar
Dash of ground cinnamon

Mix 1 tablespoon sugar and the cornstarch in 16-ounce casserole. Stir in blueberries and lemon juice. Microwave uncovered on medium-high (70%) until boiling, 2 to 3½ minutes; stir.

Mix baking mix, 1 teaspoon sugar, the milk and sour cream until soft dough forms. Drop dough by 3 spoonfuls onto hot blueberry mixture. Mix ½ teaspoon sugar and the cinnamon; sprinkle over dough. Microwave uncovered until top of dough is almost dry, 1½ to 3 minutes. Let stand uncovered 5 minutes before serving.

2 SERVINGS

2 tablespoons sugar
1 teaspoon cornstarch
1⅓ cups fresh or frozen (thawed) blueberries
2 teaspoons lemon juice
½ cup baking mix
2 teaspoons sugar
2 tablespoons milk
2 tablespoons dairy sour cream
1 teaspoon sugar
⅛ teaspoon ground cinnamon

Mix 2 tablespoons sugar and the cornstarch in 1-quart casserole. Stir in blueberries and lemon juice. Microwave uncovered on medium-high (70%) until boiling, 3½ to 6½ minutes; stir.

Mix baking mix, 2 teaspoons sugar, the milk and sour cream until soft dough forms. Drop dough by 6 spoonfuls onto hot blueberry mixture. Mix 1 teaspoon sugar and the cinnamon; sprinkle over dough. Microwave uncovered until top of dough is almost dry, 2½ to 4½ minutes. Let stand uncovered 5 minutes before serving.

Creamy Almond Pudding

1 SERVING

⅓ cup milk
1 tablespoon sugar
2 tablespoons beaten egg
1 teaspoon cornstarch
1½ teaspoons margarine or butter
⅛ teaspoon almond extract

Mix milk, sugar, egg and cornstarch in 1-cup measure until smooth. Microwave uncovered on high (100%) 45 seconds; stir. Microwave uncovered until mixture thickens and boils, 30 to 40 seconds longer. Stir in remaining ingredients. Pour into dessert dish. Serve warm or chilled.

2 SERVINGS

⅔ cup milk
2 tablespoons sugar
1 egg, beaten
2 teaspoons cornstarch
1 tablespoon margarine or butter
¼ teaspoon almond extract

Mix milk, sugar, egg and cornstarch in 2-cup measure until smooth. Microwave uncovered on high (100%) 1½ minutes; stir. Microwave uncovered until mixture thickens and boils, 40 to 50 seconds longer. Stir in remaining ingredients. Pour into 2 dessert dishes. Serve warm or chilled.

Raisin Bread Pudding

1 SERVING

Prepare Raisin Bread Pudding for 2 Servings. Cover and refrigerate 1 serving for another meal. To reheat, microwave uncovered on high (100%) until warm, 15 to 20 seconds.

2 SERVINGS

1 tablespoon margarine or butter
¾ cup milk
1 egg, beaten
2 tablespoons sugar
¼ teaspoon vanilla
2 slices raisin bread, cut into cubes
Dash of ground cinnamon

Place margarine in 2-cup measure. Microwave uncovered on high (100%) until melted, 30 to 40 seconds. Mix in milk, egg, sugar and vanilla with fork. Stir in bread. Spoon into two 10-ounce custard cups; sprinkle with cinnamon. Microwave uncovered on medium (50%) 4 minutes; rotate cups ½ turn. Microwave until almost set, 4 to 4½ minutes longer.

Lemon Berry Pound Cake

1 SERVING

Lemon Dessert Sauce (below)
¼ cup fresh berries
1 slice pound or angel food cake

Prepare Lemon Dessert Sauce. Place pound cake on serving plate. Top with berries and half of sauce. Cover and refrigerate remaining sauce for another meal.

2 SERVINGS

Lemon Dessert Sauce (below)
½ cup fresh berries
2 slices pound or angel food cake

Prepare Lemon Dessert Sauce. Place pound cake on serving plates. Top each with half of berries and sauce.

LEMON DESSERT SAUCE

2 tablespoons sugar
1 teaspoon cornstarch
¼ cup water
1 tablespoon lemon juice
½ teaspoon grated lemon peel
Dash of salt
1½ teaspoons margarine or butter

Mix sugar and cornstarch in 1-cup measure; stir in water, lemon juice, lemon peel and salt. Microwave uncovered on high (100%), stirring every 30 seconds, until thickened and boiling, 1 to 1½ minutes. Stir in margarine until smooth. Reheat sauce on medium (50%) until warm, 30 to 40 seconds.

Apricot Brandy Sundae

1 SERVING

Apricot Brandy Sauce (below)
2 slices pound cake
1 scoop vanilla ice cream

Prepare Apricot Brandy Sauce. Place pound cake and ice cream in serving dish. Top with half of sauce. Cover and refrigerate remaining sauce for another meal. Reheat sauce on medium (50%) until warm, 30 to 40 seconds.

2 SERVINGS

Apricot Brandy Sauce (below)
4 slices pound cake
2 scoops vanilla ice cream

Prepare Apricot Brandy Sauce. Place 2 slices pound cake and 1 scoop ice cream in each of 2 serving dishes. Top each with half of sauce.

APRICOT BRANDY SAUCE

¼ cup apricot preserves
1 tablespoon corn syrup
1 teaspoon lemon juice
1 tablespoon apricot-flavored brandy

Mix preserves, corn syrup, and lemon juice in 1-cup measure. Microwave uncovered on high (100%) until preserves are melted, 30 to 40 seconds. Stir in brandy.

Hot Fudge Sundae Cake

1 SERVING

Prepare Hot Fudge Sundae Cake for 2 Servings. Cover and refrigerate half of the cake for another meal.

2 SERVINGS

¼ cup all-purpose flour
3 tablespoons granulated sugar
2 teaspoons cocoa
½ teaspoon baking powder
Dash of salt
2 tablespoons milk
2 teaspoons vegetable oil
¼ teaspoon vanilla
2 tablespoons chopped nuts
¼ cup packed brown sugar
1 tablespoon cocoa
½ cup hot water
Ice cream

Mix flour, granulated sugar, 2 teaspoons cocoa, the baking powder and salt in 24-ounce casserole. Stir in milk, oil and vanilla until smooth. Stir in nuts; sprinkle with brown sugar and 1 tablespoon cocoa.

Place water in 1-cup measure. Microwave uncovered on high (100%) until boiling, 1 to 1½ minutes. Pour over batter. Microwave uncovered on high (100%) 1 minute; rotate casserole ¼ turn. Microwave uncovered until cake is set but still glossy, 1½ to 2 minutes longer. Serve warm, topped with scoops of ice cream. Garnish with sliced bananas, toasted nuts and maraschino cherries if desired.

Apricot Brandy Sundae (page 123)
and Hot Fudge Sundae Cake

Index